Grade 5

by Angela Frith Antrim,
Redeana Davis Smith, and Vicky Shiotsu

Carson-Dellosa Publishing LLC
Greensboro, North Carolina

GUINNESS WORLD RECORDS™ DISCLAIMER: Guinness World Records Limited has a very thorough accreditation system for records verification. However, while every effort is made to ensure accuracy, Guinness World Records Limited cannot be held responsible for any errors contained in this work. Feedback from our readers on any point of accuracy is always welcomed.

SAFETY DISCLAIMER: Attempting to break records or set new records can be dangerous. Appropriate advice should be taken first, and all record attempts are undertaken entirely at the participant's risk. In no circumstances will Guinness World Records Limited or Carson-Dellosa Publishing LLC have any liability for death or injury suffered in any record attempts. Guinness World Records Limited has complete discretion over whether or not to include any particular records in the annual Guinness World Records book.

Due to the publication date, the facts and the figures contained in this book are current as of July 2010.

Credits

Content Editors: Elizabeth Swenson and Heather R. Stephan
Copy Editor: Julie B. Killian
Layout and Cover Design: Van Harris

This book has been correlated to state, common core state, national, and Canadian provincial standards. Visit *www.carsondellosa.com* to search for and view its correlations to your standards.

Carson-Dellosa Publishing LLC
PO Box 35665
Greensboro, NC 27425 USA
www.carsondellosa.com

ISBN 978-1-936024-04-9

335101151

TABLE OF CONTENTS

INTRODUCTION

A man held the tails of 11 rattlesnakes in his mouth. Eight elephants painted a picture that sold for $39,000. A tailor sewed a pair of underpants that measured 40 feet from the waistband to the crotch. The largest stick insect is 22 inches long. Welcome to the wild, wacky, and amazing achievements of Guinness World Records™!

Guinness World Records is the authority on feats that are of interest to the world or have historic importance. Since the first publication of *The Guinness Book of Records* in 1955, readers have laughed, gasped, and gagged at the details. Students are especially drawn to the facts. Short, exciting, and to the point, the records open up a fascinating world to explore, in both human endeavors and nature's endless marvels.

It is a natural step to pair students' interests in world records with math. To be a record, the achievement has to have qualities that can be measured (weight, height, distance, speed, or monetary value, for example) and compared (lightest, tallest, slowest, etc.). The numbers provide endless opportunities to practice math skills and strategies in a fun way. Wow, that dog broke the record by jumping three inches higher! The biggest spider could fill my dinner plate! I like roller coasters, so riding one for 405 consecutive hours would be fun. But, wait! That's nearly 17 days!

MAKING GUINNESS WORLD RECORDS™

Guinness World Records accomplishments are facts that belong in one of eight categories:

- Human Body
- Amazing Feats
- Natural World
- Science and Technology
- Arts and Media
- Modern Technology
- Travel and Transport
- Sports and Games

Some records are new because they are exciting and involve events that have never been attempted. People with unique talents are also permitted to become record-makers. However, most of the record events are established, and people try to find the ones that they can break.

Guinness World Records receives more than 60,000 requests per year. Record-makers and breakers must apply first so that their attempts are official. The organization sets guidelines for each event to make sure that it can be properly measured. Guinness World Records also makes sure that record-breakers follow the same steps so that each participant gets an equal chance. Professional judges make sure that the guidelines are followed correctly and measured accurately. However, the guidelines may designate other community members who can serve as judges to witness an event. Once the record attempt is approved, the participant gets a framed certificate. The person's name may also be included in the yearly publication or on the Guinness World Records Web site at *www.guinnessworldrecords.com*.

World Record Themes

Guinness World Records™ Math is divided into five themes, each focusing on 10 to 14 exciting records:

- Amazing Animals
- Earth Extremes
- Wild, Wacky & Weird
- Engineering, Science & the Body
- Game Time!

Math Passages

Each left page features a reading passage about a remarkable world record. This engaging, high-interest passage recounts numeric and human-interest details of the record. A box on each reading passage page provides more amazing records relating to the featured record-maker or record-breaker. Leveled writing ensures success for all students. An eye-popping color photograph of the accomplishment accompanies each passage to support the content.

Math Word Problems

On each right page, five to six word problems focus students' attention on the details of the records, allowing students to practice math skills in a real-world application. Formats include fill-in-the-blank, multiple choice, matching comparisons, and tables, graphs, and charts. Problems increase in difficulty and include a variety of math strands and cognitive levels. Nearly every page provides practice in critical thinking skills and mixed measurement conversions.

BE A RECORD-BREAKER!

Hey, kids!

At age 10, Tiana Walton put 27 gloves on her hand. Mark Aldridge was 17 when he popped 56 balloons with the end of his pogo stick in one minute. Eighty-five-year-old Saul Moss went scuba diving in the ocean. So, why are these people important? They are Guinness World Records™ record-makers and record-breakers! Walton, Aldridge, and Moss did something truly amazing!

A world record is a weird, wacky, or amazing achievement that is a fact. It can be a skill someone has, such as popping the most balloons with a pogo stick, or it can be an interesting part of nature, such as the smelliest bird. Guinness World Records has judges who set rules to make sure that all record-makers and record-breakers follow the same steps. Then, the judges count, weigh, measure, and compare to make sure that the achievement is the greatest in the world.

So, can you be a Guinness World Records record-breaker? If you can run, hop, toss, or even race with an egg on a spoon, you just might see your name on a record. With the help of an adult, visit *www.guinnessworldrecords.com*. There you will find a world of exciting records to explore— and maybe break!

 The Carson-Dellosa Team

SKILLS MATRIX

Page Number	Algebra	Data Analysis	Estimation	Geometry	Measurement	Number & Operations	Time
11	✔		✔		✔	✔	
13	✔	✔			✔	✔	
15	✔	✔			✔	✔	✔
17					✔	✔	✔
19			✔	✔	✔	✔	
21	✔		✔		✔	✔	
23			✔		✔	✔	✔
25		✔	✔		✔	✔	
27	✔	✔	✔		✔	✔	✔
29	✔	✔	✔	✔	✔	✔	✔
31		✔		✔	✔	✔	✔
33		✔	✔		✔	✔	✔
35		✔	✔			✔	✔
37	✔			✔	✔	✔	✔
39	✔				✔	✔	
41			✔		✔	✔	✔
43			✔		✔	✔	✔
45	✔	✔	✔	✔	✔	✔	✔
47		✔		✔	✔	✔	
49		✔	✔		✔	✔	
51			✔		✔	✔	✔
53	✔		✔	✔	✔	✔	✔
55	✔		✔		✔	✔	✔
57			✔			✔	✔
59	✔				✔	✔	✔
61					✔	✔	✔
63			✔		✔	✔	✔
65		✔			✔	✔	✔
67	✔			✔	✔	✔	
69	✔		✔		✔	✔	

Page Number	Algebra	Data Analysis	Estimation	Geometry	Measurement	Number & Operations	Time
71	✔					✔	
73	✔		✔	✔	✔	✔	✔
75		✔	✔	✔	✔	✔	
77	✔	✔		✔	✔	✔	✔
79	✔		✔		✔	✔	✔
81			✔		✔	✔	✔
83	✔				✔	✔	
85	✔	✔	✔		✔	✔	✔
87	✔		✔	✔	✔	✔	
89		✔	✔		✔	✔	
91	✔	✔	✔		✔	✔	
93		✔		✔	✔	✔	
95			✔		✔	✔	
97	✔		✔		✔	✔	
99	✔		✔		✔	✔	
101	✔	✔			✔	✔	
103	✔	✔	✔	✔	✔	✔	✔
105	✔	✔	✔	✔	✔		✔
107	✔		✔	✔		✔	✔
109	✔		✔	✔	✔	✔	✔
111		✔		✔	✔	✔	✔
113	✔	✔	✔	✔	✔	✔	✔
115			✔		✔	✔	✔
117		✔			✔	✔	✔
119	✔		✔		✔	✔	
121			✔		✔	✔	✔
123		✔	✔	✔	✔	✔	✔
125						✔	✔

A PAIR OF CHAMPIONS

■ Check this out!
Heaviest Dog Breed

The Old English mastiff and the St. Bernard share a special title. They are the heaviest dogs in the world. The males of both species weigh around 170 to 200 pounds. That is heavier than many grown men! The St. Bernard can be up to 30 inches tall at the shoulders. The Old English mastiff is slightly taller and can be up to 32 inches tall at the shoulders. With their large heads and powerful bodies, these dogs are true heavyweight champions!

MORE AMAZING RECORDS

Smallest Domestic Hamster Breed: The smallest breed of hamster is the Roborovski hamster. It is just 1.5 to 2 inches long!

Longest Rabbit: The Longest Rabbit is Darius, a Flemish giant rabbit owned by Annette Edwards (UK). Darius measured 4 feet 3 inches long on April 6, 2010.

Most Expensive Cat: The Most Expensive Cat was a California spangled cat that was included in the 1986 Neiman Marcus Christmas Book. The cat sold for $24,000 in January 1987.

Name_____ Date_____

■ Answer the questions. Show your work.

1. How many 25-pound cocker spaniels would equal the weight of one 200-pound Old English mastiff?

2. How much longer is the world's Longest Rabbit than the height of a St. Bernard?

3. Is the Old English mastiff taller or shorter than 3/4 of a yard? Explain your thinking.

4. Which is the best estimate for the weight of an Old English mastiff and a St. Bernard altogether?

    A. 100 to 170 pounds

    B. 200 to 300 pounds

    C. 340 to 400 pounds

    D. 400 to 550 pounds

5. If 1 of the world's Smallest Domestic Hamsters is 1.5 inches long, how many hamsters standing head to toe would equal the height of a St. Bernard?

6. Suppose you have 2 St. Bernards and 1 Old English mastiff. Each dog weighs more than 190 pounds but less than 200 pounds. The 3 dogs have different weights. If they weigh 577 pounds in all, what is the weight of each dog?

KING OF THE NORTH

■ Check this out!

Largest Carnivore on Land

Can you guess which Arctic animal is the most powerful? If you guessed the polar bear, you would be right! The polar bear is the largest of all land carnivores or meat-eaters. An average adult male polar bear weighs around 880 to 1,320 pounds. From his nose to his tail measures up to 8 feet 6 inches long! Although a polar bear's fur looks white, each of his hairs is actually clear and hollow. The hair reflects the sun's rays, making the fur look white. This helps hide the bear as he travels across snow and ice in search of food. This King of the North is also an excellent swimmer. Polar bears are known to swim more than 60 miles to find a meal!

MORE AMAZING RECORDS

Smallest Carnivore: The world's Smallest Carnivore is the dwarf, or least, weasel. From its head to the end of its body, it is 4.3 to 10.2 inches long. Its tail is 0.5 to 3.4 inches long, and its weight is 1 to 7 ounces.

Smallest Primate: Primates are mammals that have large brains, grasping hands, and forward-facing eyes. The world's Smallest Primate is the pygmy mouse lemur. From its head to the end of its body, it is about 2.4 inches long. Its tail is 5.4 inches long, and its average weight is just 1.1 ounces.

Largest Nocturnal Primate: The world's Largest Nocturnal (active at night) Primate is the aye-aye of Madagascar. It has a body length of 16 inches, a tail length of 20 inches, and a weight of about 6 pounds.

Name_____ Date_____

■ Answer the questions. Show your work.

1. Complete the sentence with **greater than**, **less than**, or **equal to**.

A polar bear that is 7 feet 10 inches long is _____ 94 inches.

2. How many of the Largest Nocturnal Primates would it take to equal the weight of one 1,320-pound polar bear?

3. What is the length of the Smallest Primate if you include its head, body, and tail?

4. If one polar bear weighs 880 pounds and another weighs 1,320 pounds, what is their mean (average) weight?

5. One polar bear swims 60 miles each week to hunt. Which equation shows how many weeks it would take him to swim 300 miles? (w = weeks)

   A. $60 + w = 300$

   B. $60w = 300$

   C. $300 - w = 60$

   D. $300 \times 60 = w$

6. One dwarf weasel is 10.2 inches long from its head to the end of its body, and its tail is 3.4 inches long. Is the total length of the weasel about 1/4, 1/8, or 1/10 the size of a polar bear measuring 8 feet 6 inches long?

A DINOSAUR'S COUSIN

■ Check this out!

Largest Crocodilian

Did you know that crocodiles and dinosaurs lived on Earth at the same time? In fact, they are relatives because they are both crocodilians! Of the two, only the crocodiles survived. Today, the world's Largest Crocodilian is the saltwater crocodile. Like its dinosaur cousins, it is a reptile. It has a long snout, short limbs, and a powerful tail. A bony coat of armor protects its body.

Adult males can weigh around 900 to 1,150 pounds. They usually grow to a length of 14 to 16 feet, but some grow to more than 20 feet. The largest known crocodile lives in a wildlife sanctuary in India and measures 23 feet long. That is more than 1/2 the length of a school bus!

MORE AMAZING RECORDS

Smallest Crocodilian: The world's Smallest Crocodilian is the dwarf caiman of northern South America. Females grow to 4 feet long, and males grow to nearly 5 feet long.

Fastest Crocodile on Land: The world's Fastest Crocodile on Land is the freshwater crocodile. It can reach a speed of 10.56 miles per hour.

Oldest Alligator: A female American alligator lived to be 66 years old. She arrived at Australia's Adelaide Zoo in June 1914 when she was 2 years old and died in September 1978.

Name_____ Date_____

■ Answer the questions. Show your work.

1. What is the speed of the Fastest Crocodile on Land rounded to the nearest tenth?

2. How much longer is the largest known crocodile than a dwarf caiman measuring 4 feet 11 inches?

3. What would be the order of the crocodiles in the chart if they were arranged from shortest to longest?

Crocodile	Length
A	15.5 feet
B	180 inches
C	$15\frac{1}{4}$ feet
D	15 feet 2 inches

4. In what year would the Oldest Alligator have been 50 years old? Explain 1 way that you can solve this problem.

5. If 2 crocodiles weigh 2,050 pounds in all, and 1 crocodile weighs 50 pounds more than the other, how much does each animal weigh? Explain your thinking.

ON YOUR MARK, GET SET, GO!

■ Check this out!
Fastest Ferret

On July 11, 1999, a pet ferret named Warhol became a racing hero. That was when he became the world's Fastest Ferret. The 6-pound Warhol won his title in a ferret racing championship. The race was held in northern England. It was the ferret's first race ever, but he ran like a pro! He dashed along a tube 32 feet 10 inches long. Cheering him on was his owner, Jacqui Adams (UK). She wasn't disappointed. Warhol ran the race in 12.59 seconds, beating 150 other racers!

MORE AMAZING RECORDS

Fastest Greyhound: The Fastest Greyhound ran 41.83 miles per hour on March 5, 1994, in Australia. It ran 400 yards in 19.57 seconds!

Fastest Chelonian: Chelonians are a group of animals that includes turtles and tortoises. A Pacific leatherback turtle set the speed for the Fastest Chelonian by traveling 22 miles per hour!

Fastest Dinosaur: Gallimimus of Mongolia was thought to be the fastest of the *Ornithomimids*. This long-legged dinosaur may have reached speeds of 25 to 37 miles per hour.

Fastest 100 Meters by a Land Mammal: On September 10, 2009, a cheetah named Sarah set a world record when she ran 100 meters in 6.13 seconds at the Cincinnati Zoo.

Name_____ Date_____

■ Answer the questions. Show your work.

1. Was Warhol's time for finishing the race closer to 12.5 seconds or 12.6 seconds? Use a number line to explain your answer.

2. What was the length of Warhol's race in inches?

3. If one of Warhol's competitors finished 1.5 seconds after Warhol, how long did it take the animal to run the race?

4. If the race were changed so that Warhol had to race down the tube and then race back to his starting point, how long would the course be?

5. What is Sarah's speed in meters per second?

6. Was the time Warhol took to run his race greater than or less than 1/4 of a minute? Explain your thinking.

HORNED SUPERSTAR

■ Check this out!

Largest Horn Circumference—Steer

Lurch became a superstar with his super-sized horns. He was an African watusi steer, which is a kind of cow. On May 6, 2003, his horns won him the title of the animal with the world's Largest Horn Circumference. The horns measured 37.5 inches around! Two veterinarians examined Lurch. They checked his horns three times to confirm their amazing size. Lurch's horns were not the longest on record, but they were still impressive. The horns had a span of 7 feet, and each one weighed more than 100 pounds!

MORE AMAZING RECORDS

Largest Duck Egg: The world's Largest Duck Egg was laid by a white Pekin duck in November 1999. The egg was 5.5 inches tall with a circumference of 8 inches and a weight of just over 8 ounces.

Largest Millipede: The Largest Millipede is an African giant black millipede. It is 15.2 inches long with a circumference of 2.6 inches. This impressive creature has 256 legs!

Largest Wasp Nest: The Largest Wasp Nest ever recorded was found on a farm in New Zealand in April 1963. It measured 12 feet 2 inches long with a diameter of 5 feet 8 inches and a circumference of 18 feet.

Name_____ Date_____

■ Answer the questions. Show your work.

1. Which fraction is equivalent to 37.5?

   A. $37\dfrac{1}{5}$ B. $37\dfrac{5}{8}$

   C. $37\dfrac{1}{2}$ D. $37\dfrac{1}{4}$

2. If you listed the circumferences of Lurch's horns, the Largest Duck Egg, the Largest Millipede, and the Largest Wasp Nest in order from smallest to largest, which one would be second?

3. Would a circle with a diameter of 10 inches have a circumference that is greater than or less than the circumference of Lurch's horns?

4. About how many Largest Duck Eggs would be needed to equal the weight of one of Lurch's horns? Explain your thinking.

5. If a person's arm span is 5 1/3 feet, how much longer is the span of Lurch's horns? Write your answer in feet and in inches.

6. About how many times greater is the span of Lurch's horns than the length of the Largest Millipede?

   4 times   **6 times**   **8 times**

WHAT A CROWD!

■ Check this out!

Largest Penguin Colony

It is crowded on Zavodovski Island in Antarctica! The island is home to the world's Largest Penguin Colony. About 2 million chinstrap penguins live there. These penguins stand 27 inches tall and weigh 9 pounds. They get their name from the thin stripe of black feathers under their chins. One million pairs of penguins can be found on the slopes of the island. From a distance, they look like little white dots against the black, volcanic earth!

MORE AMAZING RECORDS

Largest Penguin Airlift: The largest airlift of penguins took place from July 1–2, 2000. Between 15,000 and 20,000 penguins were rescued and taken by airplane after a massive oil spill struck western South Africa on June 23, 2000.

Highest Density of Feathers: The bird with the Highest Density of Feathers is the penguin. Several species have 11 to 12 feathers per square centimeter of their bodies.

Rarest Species of Penguin: The world's rarest penguin is the yellow-eyed penguin. It is found only in New Zealand. Only about 4,500 to 5,000 of these penguins are left.

Name_____ Date_____

■ **Answer the questions. Show your work.**

1. What is 2 million in standard form?
   - **A.** 200,000,000
   - **B.** 20,000,000
   - **C.** 2,000,000,000
   - **D.** 2,000,000

2. What is the value of the 5 in 15,000?

3. If 20,000 penguins were airlifted from Zavodovski Island, about how many penguins would be left?

4. If 5,000 yellow-eyed penguins in New Zealand joined the chinstrap penguins on Zavodovski Island, how many penguins would there be in all?

5. How many chinstrap penguins standing one on top of the other are needed to make a height of 9 feet? Explain your thinking.

6. Suppose 1 penguin dives into the sea, followed by 2 penguins, then 3, and so on. After the last group dives in, 55 penguins are in the water altogether. How many penguins were in the last group? Explain your thinking.

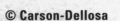

NIGHT-LIGHT

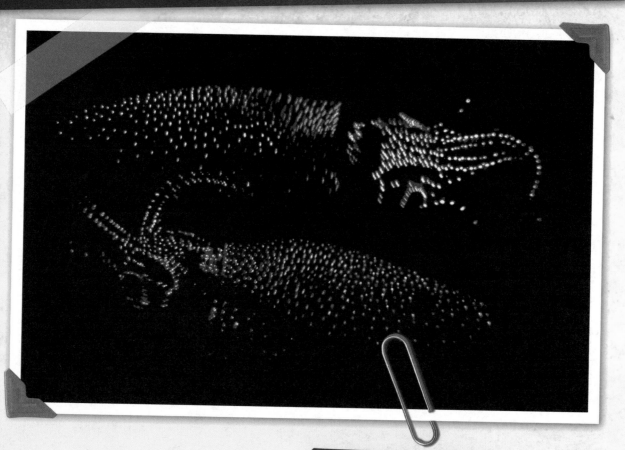

■ Check this out!

Most Bioluminescent Squid

The firefly squid lives in the western Pacific Ocean waters surrounding Japan. This small sea creature holds the Guinness World Records™ record for being the world's Most Bioluminescent Squid. *Bioluminescent* means able to produce your own light. The firefly squid reaches a mere 2.4 inches in length and tops the scales at just 0.3 ounces in weight.

Photophores, or light-producing organs, cover the squid's body and allow it to produce a brilliant blue glow. During the day, the firefly squid can be found in darkness at depths as low as 1,200 feet. At night, the squid drifts to the surface to find food before returning to its deep, dark home.

MORE AMAZING RECORDS

Most Bioluminescent Organism: The world's Most Bioluminescent Organism is the sea walnut. It grows up to 4.7 inches. Sea walnuts are a type of comb jellies that are often confused with jellyfish.

Most Dangerous Glowing Animals: Scorpions are the world's Most Dangerous Glowing Animals. All scorpions have a blue glow when under an ultraviolet light.

Most Versatile Bioluminescent Fish: Most bioluminescent fish emit light that is green-blue. But, dragonfish can emit red light, which other fish cannot see.

Largest Bioluminescent Organism: The world's Largest Bioluminescent Organism is a honey mushroom in Oregon. It covers 2,200 acres! It is believed to be at least 2,400 years old.

Name_____ Date_____

■ Answer the questions. Show your work.

1. What is the difference in length between the world's Most Bioluminescent Squid and the world's Most Bioluminescent Organism?

2. Convert the decimal measurements of the firefly squid into fraction measurements.

   Length _____   Weight _____

3. If squid were selling for $9.75 per pound, and you needed 3 pounds, how much money would you spend?

4. How many yards below the ocean's surface would you find a firefly squid during the day?

5. The world's Largest Bioluminescent Organism is at least how many days old?

6. **About** how many firefly squid would it take to equal 1 pound?

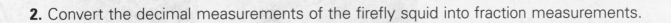

FAR-JUMPING FROG

■ Check this out!

Farthest Jump by a Frog

The record for the longest triple jump by a frog has stood since May 21, 1977. On that date, a South African sharp-nosed frog named Santjie leaped 33 feet 10 inches to set a new Guinness World Records™ record. The total distance of the jump was found by adding the lengths of 3 leaps in a row. Santjie's winning jumps covered about 1/2 of the distance of a standard basketball court!

Santjie's record was set at a frog derby at Lurula Natal Spa in Petersburg, KwaZulu-Natal, South Africa. In frog derbies, proud owners bring their pet frogs to compete in many different leaping contests in hopes of winning a prize.

MORE AMAZING RECORDS

Highest Jump by a Dog: Kate Long and Kathleen Conroy of Miami, Florida, own a dog named Cinderella May. On October 7, 2006, Cinderella May cleared a jump of 68 inches.

Highest Jump by a Kangaroo: A grey kangaroo once jumped over an 8-foot-tall fence. A red kangaroo once cleared a 10-foot-tall stack of wood!

Highest Jump by a Dolphin: Bottlenose dolphins have been trained to jump as high as 26 feet straight up from the surface of the water.

Name_____ Date_____

■ Answer the questions. Show your work.

1. The frog's 3 jumps totaled 33 feet 10 inches. If the frog jumped twice as far, how many feet and inches would it have jumped?

   A. 16 feet 11 inches

   B. 43 feet 1 inch

   C. 67 feet 8 inches

   D. 86 feet 3 inches

2. If the record-setting frog jumped a total of 33 feet 10 inches, he jumped a total

   of _____ inches.

3. Santjie's 3 leaps totaled 33 feet 10 inches. Determine the average length in feet and inches of each of the jumps. Round the answer to the nearest hundredth.

4. The grey kangaroo's record-setting jump was _____ feet _____ inches longer than Cinderella May's record-setting jump.

5. Which unit would be the best for measuring the height of the world's Highest Jump by a Kangaroo?

   A. kilometer

   B. meter

   C. centimeter

   D. millimeter

6. One mile equals 5,280 feet. If a dolphin leaps 26 feet from the surface of the water, about what portion of a mile does it jump into the air? Explain your answer.

FAR FROM FICKLE EATERS

■ Check this out!

Fastest-Eating Mammal

The star-nosed mole does not take long to find and eat its food. In fact, it holds the Guinness World Records™ record for being the Fastest-Eating Mammal in the animal kingdom.

Dr. Kenneth Catania (USA) used high-speed cameras to film the moles in slow motion. He found that star-nosed moles, on average, take 230 milliseconds to see, catch, and eat their prey. But, the moles can do this in as little as 120 milliseconds! Humans even take about 650 milliseconds to begin stopping for a stoplight when driving. Star-nosed moles have 22-point, star-shaped noses, which contain 5 times more nerves for touch than the human hand.

MORE AMAZING RECORDS

Fastest-Eating Fish: Frogfish can open their mouths and swallow their prey in less than 6 milliseconds.

Hungriest Bear Species: A giant panda must eat about 38 percent of his own weight in bamboo shoots or 15 percent of his own weight in bamboo leaves and stems each day. Because the giant panda's body only digests about 21 percent of what he eats, he must eat for about 15 hours every day!

Hungriest Birds: Hummingbirds eat about 1/2 of their body weight in food every day. The tiny bird's diet consists of small insects and nectar.

Name_____ Date_____

■ Answer the questions. Show your work.

1. Write 230 milliseconds as a decimal in seconds.

2. Which tool would be the best for measuring the amount of time it takes frogfish to eat their food? Explain your thinking.
   - **A.** stopwatch
   - **B.** high-speed camera
   - **C.** naked eye
   - **D.** analog clock

3. Write 21 percent, the amount of bamboo that a giant panda digests, as a decimal and as a fraction.

4. On 1 particular day, a group of hummingbirds ate the following amounts of food: 1.5 grams, 2 grams, 1.75 grams, 1.5 grams, 1.25 grams, and 1.8 grams. Find the mode of the data.

5. If a star-nosed mole has about 25,000 nerve endings on his nose, how many nerve endings does a human have in her hand? Write and solve an equation to find the answer.

6. About how much more quickly does a star-nosed mole react to food when compared to a human's reaction time at a stoplight? Explain your thinking.

CAREFUL . . . CAREFUL

■ Check this out!

Fastest 100 Meters with a Can Balanced on the Head by a Dog

The room grew quiet. You could almost hear a pin drop as Sweet Pea tried to break a Guinness World Records™ record. She was going for the Fastest 100 Meters with a Can Balanced on the Head. What is so special about this record? Sweet Pea is a dog! She is an Australian shepherd/border collie mix.

It was a long and quiet 2 minutes, 55 seconds for Sweet Pea's owner, Alex Rothacker (USA), on September 3, 2008. But, he could cheer when Sweet Pea broke the record! Sweet Pea is an amazing animal. She also holds 3 other Guinness World Records.

MORE AMAZING RECORDS

Most Skips by a Dog in 1 Minute: On August 8, 2007, Sweet Pea skipped a jump rope 75 times in 1 minute on live TV.

Most Steps Walked Up by a Dog Facing Forward While Balancing a Glass of Water: On August 8, 2007, Sweet Pea walked up 17 steps while balancing a glass of water on her snout.

Most Steps Walked Up by a Dog Going Backward While Balancing a Glass of Water: On January 5, 2008, Sweet Pea walked backward up 10 steps while balancing a 5-ounce glass of water in Germany.

Name_____ Date_____

■ Answer the questions. Show your work.

1. Sweet Pea balanced a glass containing 5 ounces of water on her snout. If she balanced 5 times more water, how much water would the glass contain?

2. If Sweet Pea only missed 3 out of every 78 skips while jumping rope, write a ratio to compare Sweet Pea's successful jumps to her total jumps.

3. Sweet Pea traveled about _____ meters per minute when she broke the record for the Fastest 100 Meters with a Can Balanced on the Head by a Dog.

4. Sweet Pea traveled 100 meters in about 3 minutes. Complete the table to estimate how long it would take Sweet Pea to travel each distance if she continued to travel at the same rate.

Distance	100 m	200 m	300 m	400 m
Time	3 minutes	_____	_____	_____

5. If Sweet Pea climbed steps that formed a triangle, and 2 of the angles measured 45°, determine the measurement of the third angle.

6. Which would be the longer distance for Sweet Pea to travel—100 meters or 100 yards? Explain your thinking.

FOUR-LEGGED HEROES

■ Check this out!

Most Celebrated Canine Rescuer

Barry, a St. Bernard rescue dog, spent his life patrolling the Swiss Alps. He searched for people in danger. During his 12-year career, Barry rescued more than 40 people from the cold mountains of Switzerland. Because of this, Barry holds the Guinness World Records™ record for the Most Celebrated Canine Rescuer.

Once, Barry rescued a little boy who had become buried in an avalanche of snow. After digging the boy out, the caring dog spread himself over the boy to warm him and licked the boy's face until he woke up. Amazingly, Barry then carried the child to safety. This four-legged rescuer is a real hero!

MORE AMAZING RECORDS

Most Successful Police Dog: From 1973 to 1979, Trepp, a golden retriever, helped make more than 100 arrests!

Highest Ranking Camel: Bert, a dromedary camel, is a reserve deputy sheriff for the Los Angeles County Sheriff's Department in California. Bert was born in March 1997 and weighs almost 1,770 pounds.

Smallest Police Dog: A chihuahua/rat terrier cross named Midge is the world's Smallest Police Dog. She is 11 inches tall and 23 inches long, and she weighs only 8 pounds!

■ Answer the questions. Show your work.

1. Midge is almost 1 _____ tall.

2. How many years did it take Trepp to make 100 arrests?

3. One ton equals 2,000 pounds. How many more pounds would Bert need to gain to weigh exactly 1 ton?

4. Suppose Midge, the world's Smallest Police Dog, has a dog house at the station for when she is off duty. If her dog house measures 3 feet by 4 feet, what is the total area of Midge's dog house?

5. If Barry weighed 168 pounds, how many Midges would it take to equal Barry's weight?

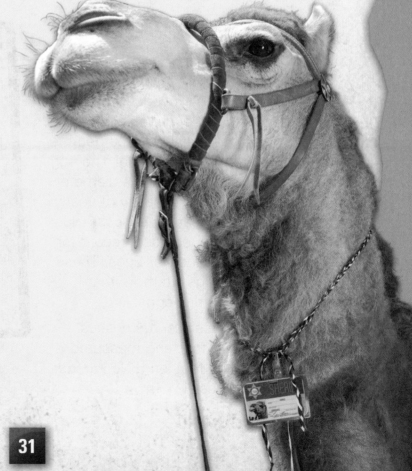

6. On average, about how many people did Barry rescue each year?

EGGS-TRAORDINARY

■ Check this out!

Largest Dinosaur Eggs

In October 1961, a fossilized dinosaur egg was found in the Provence region of France. This dinosaur egg was left by a *Hypselosaurus priscus*, which roamed the earth about 80 million years ago! The egg measured 12 inches long, had a diameter of 10 inches, and had a capacity of nearly 7 pints! The *Hypselosaurus priscus* holds the Guinness World Records™ record for having the Largest Dinosaur Eggs. These gigantic dinosaur eggs are more than twice the size of ostrich eggs.

A full-grown *Hypselosaurus priscus* weighed around 10 tons and measured between 26 and 39 feet long. No wonder its eggs were colossal!

MORE AMAZING RECORDS

Largest Fish Egg: The whale shark takes the title for having the world's Largest Fish Egg. A fisherman in the Gulf of Mexico discovered an egg measuring 12 by 5.5 by 3.5 inches in June 1953.

Largest Duck Egg: A white Pekin duck laid the world's Largest Duck Egg in 1999 in Ireland. The egg measured 5.5 inches high and had a circumference of 8 inches.

Largest Insect Egg: The Malaysian stick insect lays the world's Largest Insect Egg. It measures 1/2 inch long—about the length of a peanut.

Name_____ Date_____

■ Answer the questions. Show your work.

1. List the Largest Dinosaur Egg, Fish Egg, and Duck Egg in chronological order based on year of discovery.

2. The Largest Duck Egg measured 5.5 inches in height. Write 5.5 in word form.

3. If 3 *Hypselosaurus priscus* were standing in line, about how long would the 3 of them be altogether?
    A. between 40 feet and 47 feet
    B. between 78 feet and 80 feet
    C. between 78 feet and 117 feet
    D. between 95 feet and 105 feet

4. Below are the lengths of 7 fossilized dinosaur eggs found in a nest. Find the mode.

    12, 9, 10, 10, 12, 11, 12

5. How many cups could a *Hypselosaurus priscus* egg hold?

6. One ton equals 2,000 pounds. About how many pounds did a *Hypselosaurus priscus* weigh?

CHICKEN POWER

■ Check this out!

Highest Capacity Chicken Manure Power Station

Can chickens provide electricity to thousands of homes? In September 2008, chickens started doing just that when the world's largest biomass power plant opened. No chickens can be found at the plant though. So, what role do the chickens play? They provide the manure!

Each year, about 440,000 tons of chicken manure are used to make electricity, giving power to thousands of homes. This is about 1/3 of the yearly output of chicken manure for the Netherlands. The process gives off less greenhouse gases than spreading the manure onto fields, making this shocking form of recycling more Earth friendly.

MORE AMAZING RECORDS

Farthest Cow Chip Toss: Steve Urner (USA) holds the record for tossing a cow chip 266 feet at a festival in California in 1981.

Largest Coprolite from a Carnivore: Sometimes, dinosaur manure becomes fossilized just like bones do. Fossilized dinosaur manure is called *coprolite*. The world's Largest Coprolite from a Carnivore ever found comes from a *Tyrannosaurus rex*. The coprolite measured 19.7 inches across and weighed more than 15 pounds!

Name_____ Date_____

■ Answer the questions. Show your work.

1. The *Tyrannosaurus rex*'s coprolite measured 19.7 inches across. Write the number in expanded form.

2. The biomass power plant converts 440,000 tons of chicken manure into electricity each year. Round 440,000 to its greatest place.

3. How many years before the opening of the biomass power plant did Urner break his Guinness World Records™ record?

4. The *Tyrannosaurus rex*'s coprolite weighed 15 pounds. Which item would most likely weigh the same?
- **A.** a dictionary
- **B.** a pair of shoes
- **C.** 2 gallon jugs full of water
- **D.** a car

5. About how many yards did Urner toss a cow chip?

6. If 440,000 tons is only 1/3 of the total output of chicken manure for the Netherlands each year, what is the total output each year?

TODDLER VOLCANOES

■ Check this out!
Smallest Volcanoes

Did you know that some volcanoes are shorter than a toddler? Sand volcanoes are the world's Smallest Volcanoes. They stand less than 20 inches high. They are only a few yards wide. Unlike other volcanoes, they do not spew hot, molten rock. Instead, they eject water and sand.

A sand volcano is formed during an earthquake. The shaking causes water below the sand to push its way up. Both water and sand explode onto the surface, causing a cone-shaped volcano.

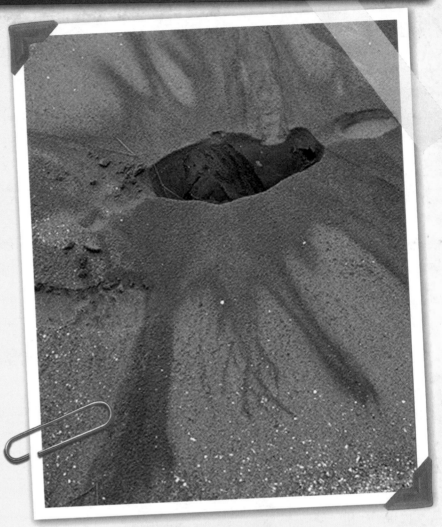

MORE AMAZING RECORDS

Tallest Volcanic Columns: Devils Tower in Wyoming is made up of the Tallest Volcanic Columns in the world. Some columns rise nearly 600 feet in the air.

Largest Volcano Crater: The world's Largest Volcano Crater is that of Toba in Sumatra, Indonesia. The Toba crater covers an area of 1,103 miles. It last erupted around 75,000 years ago.

Longest Continuously Erupting Volcano: Italy's Mount Stromboli has had continuous eruptions since at least the seventh century BC. It usually has several mild explosions each hour!

■ Answer the questions. Show your work.

1. Fifty centimeters is equal to what fraction of a meter?

2. If a sand volcano is 3.5 meters wide, what is its width in centimeters?

3. What is the height of the Tallest Volcanic Columns in yards?

4. If Mount Stromboli erupted every hour, how many hours did it continually erupt during the period of March 2010 to June 2010?

5. If in 1 hour Mount Stromboli had 6 explosions spaced equally apart, how many explosions did it have in 20 minutes? Explain your thinking.

6. If a rectangular plot of land had the same area as the area of the world's Largest Volcano Crater, what could its length and width be? Explain your thinking.

CHILI PEPPER CHAMP

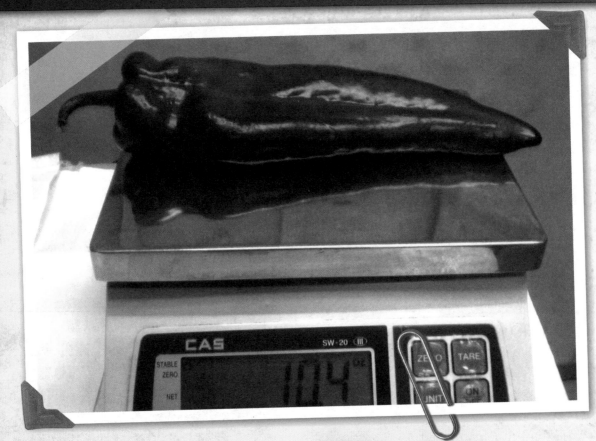

■ Check this out!

Heaviest Pepper

If there were a contest for hefty chili peppers, one pepper would be champ. That would be a green chili pepper from Pearce, Arizona. It was grown by Edward Curry (USA) on his farm. When measured in November 2009, the pepper weighed 0.64 pounds. It set a record for the world's Heaviest Pepper. The pepper's size was amazing too. Its length was 10.25 inches, and its width was 3.75 inches. The pepper was almost as big as a sheet of notebook paper folded in half lengthwise!

MORE AMAZING RECORDS

Hottest Spice: The hottest spice is the chili pepper Bhut Jolokia. It measured 1,001,304 Scoville Heat Units on September 9, 2006. Heat units show how many parts of sugar water are needed to dilute 1 part of the pepper extract until the pepper's heat can no longer be felt.

Tallest Pepper Plant: The world's Tallest Pepper Plant was grown in Irvine, California. In April 1999, the 2-year-old plant measured 16 feet tall!

Most Jalapeño Peppers Eaten in 1 Minute: In September 2006, Alfredo Hernandes (USA) ate the most jalapeño peppers in 1 minute—16!

Name_____ Date_____

■ Answer the questions. Show your work.

1. What is the value of the 2 in 10.25?

2. What is the width of the world's Heaviest Pepper rounded to the nearest whole number?

3. How many ounces equal the weight of the world's Heaviest Pepper?

4. If 100 peppers each weighed as much as the world's Heaviest Pepper, what would be their combined weight?
   - A. 64 pounds
   - B. 6.4 pounds
   - C. 0.64 pounds
   - D. 640 pounds

5. How much longer is the height of the world's Tallest Pepper Plant than the length of the world's Heaviest Pepper?

6. If Hernandes ate 16 jalapeño peppers in 1 minute at the same rate each, how long did it take for him to eat 4 of the peppers? Explain your thinking.

WHAT A LONG DAY!

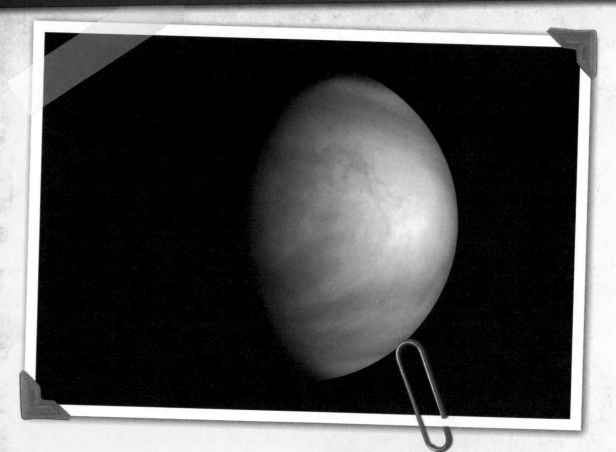

■ Check this out!
Planet with the Longest Day

Have you ever wished for more hours in the day? If you traveled to Venus, you would get your wish! Venus has the longest day of all of the planets in our solar system. One Venus day equals 243.16 Earth days. That is how long it takes the planet to rotate on its axis one time. In contrast, Earth takes 23 hours, 56 minutes, 4 seconds to complete one rotation. However, 1 year on Venus is shorter than 1 year on Earth. That is because Venus is closer to the sun. It takes 224.7 Earth days for Venus to revolve around the sun one time. That means Venus's day is longer than its year!

MORE AMAZING RECORDS
Planet with the Shortest Day: Jupiter has the shortest day of the 8 planets in our solar system. It completes one rotation on its axis every 9 hours, 55 minutes, 29.69 seconds. But, Jupiter is so far from the sun that it takes 4,332.6 Earth days to complete 1 year!

Fastest Planet: Mercury revolves around the sun in 87.9686 Earth days, with an average speed of 107,030 miles per hour. Mercury is almost twice as fast as Earth!

Farthest Planet in Our Solar System: Neptune is the farthest planet from the sun. It is 2.8 billion miles away! It travels at 3.39 miles per second and takes 164.79 Earth years to complete 1 year.

Name_____ Date_____

■ Answer the questions. Show your work.

1. Which mixed number equals 243.16?

    A. $243\dfrac{1}{10}$ **B.** $243\dfrac{16}{10}$

    C. $243\dfrac{16}{100}$ **D.** $243\dfrac{16}{1,000}$

2. In Earth days, how much longer is Venus's day than its year?

3. How far does the world's Fastest Planet travel in 1/2 hour?

4. One mile equals about 1.6 kilometers. How many kilometers is Neptune away from the sun?

5. If 1 day on Venus equals 243.16 Earth days, about how many Earth months does it equal? Round the answer to the nearest whole month.

6. Are 2 days on Jupiter longer than or shorter than 1 day on Earth? Explain your thinking.

"SNOW" FOOLING—SHE'S TALL!

■ Check this out!

Tallest Snowman

The people in Bethel, Maine, hold the record for the world's Tallest Snowman, Angus. Built in 1999, the ice king was 113 feet 7 inches tall. He weighed about 8 million pounds!

The Bethel residents knew they could do better though. So, they built Olympia, a giant snow woman. They finished building her on February 28, 2008. She stood 122 feet 1 inch tall and weighed 13,000,000 pounds. Like Angus, Olympia's arms were made with 25-foot-tall trees. She also had an 8-foot-long nose. Sadly, Olympia melted away by July 30, 2008.

MORE AMAZING RECORDS

Fastest Half Marathon Run While Barefoot on Ice or Snow: The record-setting run took 2 hours, 6 minutes, 34 seconds. The runner completed the 13-mile race in January 2007.

Highest Recorded Speed by a Snowboarder: Darren Powell (Australia) snowboarded 125.459 miles per hour in May 1999.

Largest Snow Cone: The world's Largest Snow Cone weighed 4,640 pounds and had 85 gallons of syrup. This record was set in January 2010 in Plymouth, Michigan.

Name_____ Date_____

■ **Answer the questions. Show your work.**

1. Which words express Olympia's weight?
   A. thirteen million pounds
   B. thirteen thousand pounds
   C. ten million three thousand pounds
   D. one hundred three million pounds

2. How much taller was Olympia than Angus?

3. How many tons did Olympia weigh?

4. About how many record-setting snow cones would equal the weight of Olympia?

5. To the nearest ten, estimate how many days it took Olympia to melt.

6. How many yardsticks standing end to end would be needed to measure Olympia's height?

A NATURAL WONDER

■ Check this out!

Oldest National Park

Do you enjoy exploring the outdoors and seeing animals? If so, you would probably like to visit Yellowstone National Park. It holds the record for the world's Oldest National Park. On March 1, 1872, U.S. President Ulysses S. Grant formed the world's first national park.

While Yellowstone covers parts of Wyoming, Idaho, and Montana, most of the park lies in Wyoming. It covers more than 3,470 square miles. The park crosses the Continental Divide and has mountains, lakes, canyons, and forests. Yellowstone also has nearly 300 waterfalls! It boasts more hot springs and geysers than any other region on Earth. Yellowstone is home to elk, grizzly bears, wolves, mountain lions, and eagles.

MORE AMAZING RECORDS

Tallest Geyser: The Waimangu geyser in New Zealand holds the record for the world's Tallest Geyser. Before 1904, the geyser erupted every 30 to 36 hours. Eruptions soared to a height of about 1,500 feet in 1903.

Largest Hydrothermal Explosion Crater: The Mary Bay explosion crater complex in Yellowstone National Park stretches 6,562 by 3,281 feet. It formed about 14,000 years ago in a series of hydrothermal explosions. Hydrothermal explosions happen when underground water heats up and turns into steam as it reaches the earth's surface.

Name_____ Date_____

■ Answer the questions. Show your work.

1. Yellowstone National Park consists of more than 3,470 square miles. Square miles indicate which measurement?

   A. perimeter

   B. length

   C. area

   D. volume

2. One meter is about 3 feet. About how many meters tall were the Waimangu geyser eruptions in 1903? Write an equation to explain your thinking.

3. Evan made the following table to display the number and type of animals he spotted during 1 year at Yellowstone National Park.

Animal	Number
Bears	60
Bison	150
Eagles	85
Wolves	80

   Which ratio best compares the amount of bison spotted to the amount of bears spotted?

   A. 15:8

   B. 5:2

   C. 2:1

   D. 4:3

4. The area of the Mary Bay explosion crater is

   _____ square feet.

5. About 95 percent of Yellowstone lies in Wyoming. How much of the park's 3,470 square miles are outside of Wyoming?

   A. 3,296.5 square miles

   B. 347 square miles

   C. 173.5 square miles

   D. 86.75 square miles

THE BEAST

■ Check this out!
Heaviest Cabbage

Do you have a favorite food? What about a favorite vegetable? Corn, beets, yams, beans? Cabbage, you say? A cabbage grown by Steven Hubacek of Wasilla, Alaska, holds the Guinness World Records™ record for the world's Heaviest Cabbage. Called "The Beast" by Hubacek, the winning vegetable was shown at the Alaska State Fair on September 4, 2009. The cabbage, which looked like a huge head of lettuce, weighed 127 pounds! The Beast was so large that it weighed 38.5 pounds more than its nearest competitor. The previous record was broken on September 2, 2009, when another cabbage grown by Hubacek weighed in at 125.9 pounds. It must have been hard for Hubacek to haul his cabbages to the fair that year!

MORE AMAZING RECORDS
Heaviest Broccoli: The world's Heaviest Broccoli was grown by John and Mary Evans (USA) in 1993, and it weighed 35 pounds.

Heaviest Brussels Sprout: In October 1992, Bernard Lavery (UK) grew a brussels sprout that weighed 18 pounds 4.8 ounces.

Heaviest Celery: The world's Heaviest Celery was grown by Scott and Mardie Robb (USA). It weighed 63 pounds 4.4 ounces and was presented at the Alaska State Fair on August 27, 2003.

Name_____ Date_____

■ Answer the questions. Show your work.

1. A cabbage most closely resembles which three-dimensional shape?

    A. circle

    B. cylinder

    C. sphere

    D. prism

2. Find the total weight in pounds of the cabbages that Hubacek took to the 2009 Alaska State Fair.

3. Find the total weight in ounces of the cabbages that Hubacek took to the 2009 Alaska State Fair.

4. The winning cabbage outweighed its nearest competitor by 38.5 pounds. Find the total weight in ounces of the winning cabbage and its nearest competitor.

5. Find the mean of the weights in pounds of the 3 cabbages considered in the 2009 Alaska State Fair. Round the answer to the nearest tenth.

WILD WEATHER

■ Check this out!

Heaviest Hailstones

The wind whistled, the rain poured, and nature flung hailstones from the sky. On April 14, 1986, large hailstones fell during a storm in Bangladesh. They weighed up to 2.2 pounds each! They hold the record for the world's Heaviest Hailstones.

Hail forms during strong storms when winds carry rain into very cold layers of the atmosphere. The rain then freezes into ice and bounces around in the strong winds. As the ice stays in the atmosphere, it grows into larger balls of ice. When the spheres of ice become too big to stay in the air, they fall to the ground as hail. Hailstones can range from the size of marbles to the size of baseballs.

MORE AMAZING RECORDS

Worst Damage Toll from a Hailstorm: In July 1984, a hailstorm in Germany caused $500 million in damage to trees, buildings, and vehicles. During the storm, the nearly 3-inch hailstones damaged about 70,000 buildings and 250,000 cars.

Greatest Snowfall for a Single Snowstorm: From February 13–19, 1959, 189 inches of snow fell at the Mt. Shasta Ski Bowl in California. Mt. Shasta is in northern California and rises 14,163 feet above sea level.

Worst Snowstorm Disaster—Damage Toll: A snowstorm dumped snow throughout the eastern United States from March 12–13, 1993. The storm caused $1.2 billion in damage.

Name_____ Date_____

■ Answer the questions. Show your work.

1. Write the cost of the damage caused by the 1993 snowstorm in numerical form.

2. Which unit would be the best for measuring the weight of the world's Heaviest Hailstones?
   A. gram
   B. milligram
   C. kilogram
   D. hectogram

3. If the record amount for Worst Damage Toll from a Hailstorm were doubled, about how much would that have cost?

4. How much snow fell in feet and inches during the Greatest Snowfall for a Single Snowstorm?

5. If the world's Heaviest Hailstones averaged 2.2 pounds each, approximately how many hailstones would total 74 pounds?

6. Which type of graph would be the best for comparing the damage caused by the 10 most violent storms in history? Explain your thinking.
   A. pie chart
   B. line graph
   C. bar graph
   D. stem-and-leaf plot

TO THE BAT CAVE

■ Check this out!

Largest Species of Cave-Dwelling Bat

The Bulmer's fruit bat was thought to be extinct and known only through 9,000-year-old fossils. A discovery in 1977 proved this to be wrong. Modern-day preserved bats were unexpectedly found, proving that this large cave dweller lived longer than was first thought. Amazingly, live Bulmer's fruit bats were later discovered thriving in a gigantic cave in a New Guinea mountain range. The bat once thought to be gone forever somehow beat the odds and now holds a place in the Guinness World Records™ record book as the world's Largest Species of Cave-Dwelling Bat.

MORE AMAZING RECORDS

Tallest Natural Cave Column: The world's Tallest Natural Cave Column is just over 200 feet tall and is located in a cave in Thailand. It was created when a stalactite (which hangs from the ceiling) and a stalagmite (which rises from the floor) connected, creating one column.

Deepest Cave: The country of Georgia is home to Krubera Cave, where explorers descended 7,188 feet 4 inches to reach the record depth.

Deepest Descent into an Ice Cave: In 1998, Janot Lamberton (France) descended 663 feet into an ice cave in Greenland.

Adult female wingspans of this large mammal can reach a width of more than 3 feet. These cave dwellers weigh approximately 21 ounces. How would you like to meet a Bulmer's fruit bat while cave exploring?

Name_____ Date_____

■ Answer the questions. Show your work.

1. About how far did explorers descend to reach the record depth for Deepest Cave? Round the answer to the nearest thousand.

2. How many years before Lamberton descended into the ice cave were more current preserved specimens of Bulmer's fruit bats found?

3. An adult female Bulmer's fruit bat weighs 1 pound _____ ounces.

4. About how many inches is the wingspan of an adult female Bulmer's fruit bat?

5. Estimate how many yards tall the world's Tallest Natural Cave Column is.

6. If 7 Bulmer's fruit bats were flying in a line side by side, wings expanded, estimate how many feet long the line would be.

TREE TRANSPLANT

■ Check this out!
Largest Tree Transplanted

Have you ever moved a houseplant into a new pot or replanted a bush? It can be hard work. But, that is nothing compared to this record. The world's Largest Tree Transplanted weighs more than 916,000 pounds!

The oak tree, named Old Glory, is about 180 to 230 years old. Old Glory stands 58 feet tall, and its branches span 104 feet wide. The trunk measures more than 16 feet in circumference!

Because of a road-widening project, Senna Tree Company (USA) moved Old Glory 0.25 miles to a new park in Los Angeles, California, on January 20, 2004. The tree was transplanted at a whopping cost of $1 million!

MORE AMAZING RECORDS

Oldest Living Tree: The roots of a 13-foot-tall spruce tree in Sweden show that it has been growing for 9,550 years, making it the world's Oldest Living Tree.

Fastest Growing Individual Tree: On June 17, 1974, an *Albizzia facata* tree was planted in Malaysia. In 13 months, it grew an astounding 35 feet, 2.8 inches!

Largest Permanent Tree Maze: Designed by Erik and Karen Poulsen (Denmark), Samsø Labyrinth covers an area of 645,835 square feet, has 16,830 feet of tree-lined passages, and includes 50,000 trees.

Name_____ Date_____

■ Answer the questions. Show your work.

1. One mile equals 1.6 kilometers. How many kilometers was Old Glory moved?

2. The maze has 16,830 feet of tree-lined passages. Write the number in expanded form.

3. In what month and year did the world's Fastest Growing Individual Tree set its record?

4. It cost $1 million to move Old Glory. About how much per pound did the move cost?

5. The world's Largest Permanent Tree Maze has an area of 645,835 square feet. If the maze were a rectangle, which formula would you use to find the area? (l = length, w = width)
   A. l + w + l + w
   B. 2(l + w)
   C. l x w
   D. 2l + 2w

6. Estimate in inches how much the *Albizzia facata* tree grew each month. Explain your thinking.

PIECE OF CAKE

■ Check this out!

Largest Cupcake

What weighed 1,315 pounds, holds a Guinness World Records™ record, and would satisfy anyone's sweet tooth? The world's Largest Cupcake! This cupcake broke the world record on October 3, 2009, at a charity concert in Boca Raton, Florida.

The recipe for this sweet treat called for an amazing 340 pounds of sugar, 346 pounds of eggs, and 75 pounds of butter! After the bakers mixed all of the ingredients together and baked the cupcake for 24 hours, it was ready to be measured. The chocolate-flavored dessert measured a jaw-dropping 6 feet wide and 4.5 feet tall!

MORE AMAZING RECORDS

Largest Fruitcake: The world's Largest Fruitcake was baked in Bucharest, Romania, on December 28, 2008. It weighed in at 619 pounds 12 ounces.

Largest Cheesecake: The world's Largest Cheesecake topped the scales at a whopping 4,704 pounds. This colossal dessert, baked in Mexico on January 25, 2009, had 1,764 pounds of cream cheese in it!

Largest Wildlife Cake: The world's largest bird seed cake weighed 2,843 pounds 15 ounces. It was more than 6 feet wide!

Name_____ Date_____

■ Answer the questions. Show your work.

1. The world's Largest Cupcake weighed 1,315 pounds. Write the number in word form.

2. Which dessert weighed the most?
   A. world's Largest Fruitcake
   B. world's Largest Cupcake
   C. world's Largest Cheesecake
   D. world's Largest Wildlife Cake

3. How many days after the fruitcake was baked was the cheesecake baked?

4. The world's Largest Fruitcake weighed 619 pounds 12 ounces. Round this weight to the nearest 100 pounds.

5. How much would the world's Largest Cupcake weigh if the recipe were tripled? Write an equation to explain your thinking.

6. If the world's Largest Cupcake recipe were doubled, how many pounds of eggs would be needed for the recipe?

A PAPER-FOLDING EXPERT

■ Check this out!

Fastest Time to Make 100 Origami Cranes

Hiromi Ashlin (Australia) is an artist and an origami expert. Origami is the Japanese art of paper folding. Ashlin often folds paper to make graceful, long-necked birds called cranes. On October 12, 2007, Ashlin set the world's Fastest Time to Make 100 Origami Cranes. Her time was 1 hour, 14 minutes, 25 seconds. She narrowly beat Keiko Kokofu, who took 1 hour, 22 minutes, 10 seconds to make the same number.

In Japan, the crane is a symbol of good luck. It is said that if you fold 1,000 paper cranes, you will get a wish. Ashlin says that she has made more than 30,000 paper cranes. That is a lot of wishes for her to make!

MORE AMAZING RECORDS

Fastest Mile of Pennies: The fastest time to lay down a mile of pennies is 2 hours, 16 minutes, 9 seconds. The Burnt Hickory Youth Ministry of Marietta, Georgia, set this record on August 2, 2008.

Fastest Time to Type 1 to 1 Million: The world's Fastest Time to Type 1 to 1 million in words is 16 years, 7 months! Les Stewart of Queensland, Australia, accomplished this feat on December 7, 1998.

Fastest Spelling Backward of 50 Words: The world's fastest time to spell 50 words backward is 2 minutes, 21 seconds. Deborah Prebble (UK) set this record in London, United Kingdom, on April 2, 2007.

Name_____ Date_____

■ Answer the questions. Show your work.

1. How many minutes did Ashlin take to make 100 paper cranes? Round the answer to the nearest whole minute.

2. If Ashlin made 30,000 paper cranes, how many wishes could she make according to the Japanese legend?

3. Fill in the blank with the whole number that makes the most sense.

Ashlin completed the paper cranes about _____ minutes faster than Kokofu.

4. How many months did it take to set the world record for typing the numbers 1 to 1 million in words?

5. How much longer did it take to lay down the world's Fastest Mile of Pennies than it did to set the world record for making 100 origami cranes?

6. If pennies were laid down at a steady rate to set the record for the world's Fastest Mile of Pennies, how long did it take to lay down 1/2 of a mile of pennies? Explain your thinking.

A HIGH-WIRE BIRTHDAY

■ Check this out!

Oldest Tightrope Walker

If it were your birthday, how would you spend the day? William Ivy Baldwin (USA) spent his 82nd birthday walking a tightrope! He did this on July 31, 1948. On that day, Baldwin became the world's Oldest Tightrope Walker. He crossed part of the Eldorado Canyon in Colorado. Below him was a drop of 125 feet. Baldwin walked across a 320-foot length of wire before a crowd of 3,000 people. It was a thrilling day—for both Baldwin and his fans!

MORE AMAZING RECORDS

Highest Aerial Trapeze Act: Mike Howard (UK) performed the Highest Aerial Trapeze Act in the world in August 1995. He walked across a beam from one hot air balloon to another at a height of 19,600 to 20,300 feet above the ground!

Longest Tightrope Crossing by Bicycle: The world's Longest Tightrope Crossing by Bicycle is 235 feet. Nik Wallenda (USA) set this world record in October 2008.

Longest Tightrope Crossed: The world's Longest Tightrope Crossed was 11,368 feet 1.32 inches long. Henri Rochetain (France) set this world record in July 1969.

Name_____ Date_____

■ Answer the questions. Show your work.

1. In what year was William Ivy Baldwin born?

2. Which metric unit would be the best for measuring the length of Baldwin's tightrope?

    A. liter

    B. meter

    C. kilogram

    D. kilometer

3. What is a drop of 125 feet in inches?

4. Complete the following expanded form that describes the length in feet of the world's Longest Tightrope Crossed.

$$11,368 = 10,000 + \underline{\hspace{2cm}} + \underline{\hspace{2cm}} + 60 + \underline{\hspace{2cm}}$$

5. If 1/5 of the people who watched Baldwin set his record were children, how many children were there?

6. Suppose a frog was at the bottom of the canyon watching Baldwin. If the frog jumped up 21 feet and fell back 1 foot each time, how many jumps would it take for the frog to leap out of the canyon? Explain your thinking.

UNICYCLE ADVENTURER

■ Check this out!

Longest Jump on a Unicycle

Imagine riding a bike with only one wheel across a rocky path or down a steep hill. That is the kind of adventure David Weichenberger (Austria) likes. Weichenberger is a unicycle champion.

Weichenberger became interested in unicycles in 1995. He has competed in and has won many events. On September 16, 2006, Weichenberger jumped 9 feet 8 inches on his unicycle. That was the Longest Jump on a Unicycle in the world!

Weichenberger coaches people who want to ride unicycles. He also takes them on what he calls "adventure trips." He says unicycling "is an awesome chance to get to know one's limits."

MORE AMAZING RECORDS

Most Bowls Caught on the Head While Riding a Unicycle: Nancy Huey (USA), an acrobat, caught and stacked 31 bowls on her head while riding a unicycle in August 1999. The unicycle was 7 1/2 feet tall, and Huey's head was more than 10 feet above the ground.

Longest Continuous Ride on a Unicycle: Sam Wakeling (UK) covered 105.57 miles on a unicycle without his feet touching the ground on September 29, 2007.

Most Stairs Climbed on a Unicycle: Benjamin Guiraud (France) climbed 670 stairs on a unicycle without any part of his body touching the ground. He performed this feat in 22 minutes, 32 seconds at the Eiffel Tower in Paris, France, on November 20, 2006.

■ Answer the questions. Show your work.

1. What is the length of Weichenberger's jump expressed as a mixed number?

   A. $9\frac{1}{2}$ feet   **B.** $9\frac{3}{4}$ feet

   C. $9\frac{3}{8}$ feet   **D.** $9\frac{2}{3}$ feet

2. What is the length of Weichenberger's jump in inches?

3. How many years passed from the time Weichenberger became interested in unicycles to when he made his longest jump? How many days was that?

4. In 2006, 2 unicycle records were set—one on September 16 and the other on November 20. How many days passed from one event to the other?

5. Suppose you rode a unicycle and jumped 1/2 the distance that Weichenberger did. Complete the following sentence with **greater than**, **equal to**, or **less than**.

   My jump would be _____ 4 feet 9 inches.

6. How much longer was Weichenberger's jump than the height of Huey's unicycle? Answer in 2 different ways, such as with and without fractions.

GREAT BALL OF PLASTIC WRAP!

■ Check this out!
Largest Ball of Plastic Wrap

Do you like to play ball? Well, 7-year-old Jake Lonsway (USA) took playing ball to a new level. He rolled the world's Largest Ball of Plastic Wrap.

In October 2006, Lonsway started with a softball-sized ball of plastic wrap. After only 8 months, Lonsway's ball of plastic wrap broke the world record. The ball stood 11.5 feet high and weighed 281.5 pounds. That is almost 5 times more than Lonsway weighs!

Lonsway wanted to break some kind of record. So his parents looked at the *Guinness World Records* book. They wanted to find a record that Lonsway could try to beat. They found the record for the ball of plastic wrap. At that time, the record was nearly 250 pounds. Soon after that, Lonsway's mother brought home a ball of plastic wrap the size of a softball. The rest is history!

MORE AMAZING RECORDS

Largest Aluminum Foil Ball: In 1987, Richard Roman (USA) made the world's Largest Aluminum Foil Ball. It weighed 1,615 pounds!

Largest Ball of Human Hair: The Largest Ball of Human Hair is 4 feet high and weighs 167 pounds. Henry Coffer (USA) is a barber and has collected hair for more than 50 years!

Largest Rubber Band Ball: The Largest Rubber Band Ball measures about 6 feet 3 inches high and weighs about 8,200 pounds. Joel Waul (USA) used 700,000 rubber bands of all sizes to make the ball.

Name_____ Date_____

■ Answer the questions. Show your work.

1. In what month and year did Lonsway's ball of plastic wrap set the Guinness World Records™ record?

2. Order the 4 balls from the records on page 62 from lightest to heaviest.

3. How much more does Lonsway's ball of plastic wrap weigh than the Largest Ball of Human Hair?

    A. 114.5 pounds

    B. 126.5 pounds

    C. 164.8 pounds

    D. 448.5 pounds

4. About how many pounds does Lonsway weigh?

5. How much taller is Lonsway's ball of plastic wrap than the Largest Rubber Band Ball?

6. Which do you think would weigh more—a 12-foot ball of plastic wrap or a 12-foot ball of human hair? Explain your thinking.

WHAT'S ON YOUR HEAD?

■ Check this out!

Heaviest Car Balanced on the Head

John Evans (UK) entertains people by setting heavy objects on his head. He has balanced 429 full soft drink cans. He has carried 36 bricks. Evans has even dangled people from his head!

His most amazing and dangerous feat, though, involved a car. On May 24, 1999, he placed a modified Mini Cooper car on his head. The car weighed 352 pounds! Evans set a Guinness World Records™ record for the Heaviest Car Balanced on the Head. He was able to balance the car for 33 seconds!

MORE AMAZING RECORDS

Heaviest Elephant Lifted: While performing in a circus in 1975, Khalil Oghaby (Iran) lifted an elephant off the ground using a harness and a platform. The animal weighed 2 tons!

Heaviest Fish Caught: The Heaviest Fish Caught in the world was a great hammerhead shark. It weighed 1,280 pounds! Bucky Dennis (USA) caught the shark in Florida in May 2006.

Heaviest Truck Pulled by Arm: The heaviest truck pulled with an arm-wrestling move weighed 16,998 pounds. Reverend Kevin Fast (Canada) set this world record in 2008.

Name_____ Date_____

■ Answer the questions. Show your work.

1. How many ounces is the world's Heaviest Car Balanced on the Head?

2. Which number is closest to 33 seconds? Explain your thinking.

$\dfrac{1}{4}$ minute $\dfrac{1}{2}$ minute   **1 minute**

3. What is the difference in weight between the world's Heaviest Fish Caught and the world's Heaviest Car Balanced on the Head?

4. If 1 canned soft drink costs 40¢, how much would all of the cans Evans balanced on his head cost in all?

5. If each brick weighs 5 pounds, and each soft drink can weighs 1/2 pound, which would weigh more—36 bricks or 429 soft drink cans? How many pounds heavier or lighter would they be?

6. How many people, bricks, and soft drink cans would you need to equal the weight of the car Evans placed on his head? Use the weights in the chart.

Person	150 pounds
Brick	5 pounds
Soft Drink Can	$\dfrac{1}{2}$ pound

YOU'LL FLIP OVER THIS PANCAKE!

■ Check this out!

Largest Pancake

Do you like pancakes? If so, you would flip over the one made on August 13, 1994. On that day, some people in Manchester, United Kingdom, cooked a huge pancake. In fact, they set a record for the Largest Pancake in the world! The pancake's diameter was 49 feet 3 inches. Its weight was an amazing 6,614 pounds! It took 5,966.4 pounds of pancake mix and 1,074.7 gallons of water to make the batter. The pancake cooked for 4 hours in a pan that was 50 feet wide. This record-setting pancake had a whopping 2 million calories!

MORE AMAZING RECORDS

Largest Cinnamon Roll: The world's Largest Cinnamon Roll weighed 246.5 pounds. The House of Bread in Mill Creek, Washington, made it on October 15, 2005.

Largest Cake: The world's Largest Cake weighed 128,089 pounds! It was made in Fort Payne, Alabama, on October 18, 1989. It included 16,204 pounds of icing, 33,826 pounds of cake flour, and 25,408 pounds of sugar. The cake was 80 feet long and 32 feet wide!

Largest Ice-Cream Sundae: The world's Largest Ice-Cream Sundae weighed 54,917 pounds. It was made in Edmonton, Alberta, in 1988.

Name_____ Date_____

■ Answer the questions. Show your work.

1. What is the radius of the pan in which the world's Largest Pancake was cooked?

2. Arrange the numbers in order from the least to the greatest.

   128,089   **16,209**   **33,826**   **25,408**

3. One ton equals 2,000 pounds. How many tons was the Largest Pancake in the world? Round the answer to the nearest whole ton.

4. If 1 person needs about 2,000 calories each day, how many people would the world's Largest Pancake provide with enough calories for a day?

5. Which equation would you use to find how much more the world's Largest Pancake weighed than the world's Largest Cinnamon Roll? (n equals the difference in weight.)
   - **A.** $6,614 \div n = 246.5$
   - **B.** $6,614 - n = 246.5$
   - **C.** $246.5 \times n = 6,614$
   - **D.** $n - 246.5 = 6,614$

6. Would the area of the world's Largest Cake be greater than or less than the area of a 50-foot square cake? Explain your thinking.

A MEATY FEAT

■ Check this out!

Longest Hot Dog

Can you imagine a hot dog that stretches longer than a football field? A hot dog made in Monterrey, Mexico, did exactly that. In September 2008, it was crowned the Longest Hot Dog in the world. It was 375.07 feet long! The meat weighed 77 pounds. The bun was heavy too. It was made from 297 pounds of flour, 33 pounds of sugar, 200 eggs, and more! Later, the hot dog was cut into 1,000 pieces. The pieces were shared with the hundreds of people who had come to see the record-setting hot dog.

MORE AMAZING RECORDS

Longest Ice-Cream Dessert: The world's Longest Ice-Cream Dessert was a sundae made in Brunswick, Georgia, in November 2009. The sundae was 130 feet 6 inches long!

Largest Hamburger Commercially Available: As of May 2009, the world's Largest Hamburger Commercially Available is sold at Mallie's Sports Grill & Bar in Southgate, Michigan. The beefy burger weighs 185.5 pounds and costs $499!

Largest Fish Cake: The world's Largest Fish Cake was made in Lincolnshire, United Kingdom, in October 2003. It weighed 80.79 pounds and measured 28.54 feet long.

Name_____ Date_____

■ Answer the questions. Show your work.

1. How many dozen eggs would you need to buy in order to get 200 eggs?

2. What is 375.07 written as a mixed number?

3. Which is the best estimate for describing the cost of the world's Largest Hamburger Commercially Available?

   A. 200 pounds for $500   **B.** 100 pounds for $500
   C. 180 pounds for $400   **D.** 150 pounds for $600

4. How much longer is the world's Longest Hot Dog than the world's Longest Ice-Cream Dessert?

5. If it took 33 pounds of sugar to make the bun for the world's Longest Hot Dog, what fraction of the bun would 11 pounds of sugar make? Explain your thinking.

6. If the world's Longest Hot Dog was cut into 1,000 pieces, would the length of each piece be more than or less than 1/2 foot? Explain your thinking.

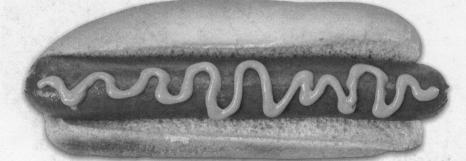

ROCKIN' FOR A GOOD CAUSE

■ Check this out!

Most Expensive Guitar Sold at Auction

How much would you pay for a guitar? Some people have paid thousands of dollars! However, that is still a bargain compared to the price of the world's Most Expensive Guitar Sold at Auction. An electric guitar that was signed by several famous rock musicians sold in November 2005 at an auction. Artists including Mick Jagger and Paul McCartney had signed the guitar. The auction was for a good cause. The guitar was sold to raise funds for a charity to help tsunami victims. It sold for $2.7 million!

MORE AMAZING RECORDS

Most Expensive Bottle of Water Sold at Auction: In November 2008, the world's Most Expensive Bottle of Water Sold at Auction sold for $23,000! The money aided the Dubai Autism Center in the United Arab Emirates.

Most Expensive Pet Home: Built in England in 2008, the world's Most Expensive Pet Home is named Barkingham Palace. It cost $384,623 to build!

Most Expensive Board Game: The world's Most Expensive Board Game is the deluxe version of *Outrage!* It costs $13,600 and includes gold and diamonds.

Most Expensive Hamburger: The Most Expensive Hamburger is called *The Burger*. It cost $186 at a fast food restaurant in the United Kingdom in 2008.

Name_____ Date_____

■ Answer the questions. Show your work.

1. Is 2.7 million closer to 2 million or 3 million?

2. What is 2.7 million in standard form?

3. How much more is the cost of the world's Most Expensive Bottle of Water Sold at Auction than the world's Most Expensive Board Game?

4. If you paid for the world's Most Expensive Bottle of Water with 100-dollar bills, how many bills would you need?

5. Suppose you have 50-dollar, 20-dollar, 10-dollar, 5-dollar, and 1-dollar bills. What is the least number of bills you could use to pay for the world's Most Expensive Hamburger?

6. If 2 people split the cost of the world's Most Expensive Hamburger, but 1 person pays 10 dollars more than the other, how much does each person pay? Explain your thinking.

MAY I HAVE A SLICE OF PIZZA?

■ Check this out!

Largest Pizza Base Spun in 2 Minutes

Around and around the pizza maker tosses the dough. He spins it until it is just the right size. At a pizzeria, a large pizza is usually 16 inches in diameter. Tony Gemignani (USA), though, spun a pizza base more than twice that size! In April 2006, he set a Guinness World Records™ record. He made the Largest Pizza Base Spun in 2 Minutes. The pizza base contained 17.6 ounces of dough, and it had a diameter of 33.2 inches. That is one big pizza!

MORE AMAZING RECORDS

Most Pizza Rolls across the Shoulder in 30 Seconds: The Most Pizza Rolls across the Shoulder in 30 Seconds using 20 ounces of dough is 37. Tony Gemignani (USA) set this world record in April 2006 in Minneapolis, Minnesota.

Largest Pizza: The world's Largest Pizza weighed 26,874 pounds. It was made in Norwood, South Africa, in December 1990.

Highest Pizza Toss: The world's Highest Pizza Toss is 21 feet 5 inches. Joe Carlucci (USA) set this record in Minneapolis, Minnesota, in April 2006.

Most Pizzas Made in 1 Hour: The Most Pizzas Made in 1 hour is 142. Donald Mark Rush (USA) made the record-setting pizzas in Mississippi in August 2008.

Name_____ Date_____

■ Answer the questions. Show your work.

1. How many seconds equal 2 minutes?

2. Is 33.2 inches greater than or less than 3 feet? How
   many inches greater than or less than 3 feet is it?

3. What is the circumference of the Largest Pizza Base
   Spun in 2 Minutes?
   - **A.** 66.4 inches
   - **B.** 104.2 inches
   - **C.** 132.8 inches
   - **D.** 332 inches

4. If 1 pepperoni pizza weighs 2.7 pounds, about how many pepperoni pizzas would
   it take to equal the weight of the world's Largest Pizza? Round the answer to the
   nearest thousand.

5. If the world's Largest Pizza Base Spun in
   2 Minutes were cut into 4 equal pieces,
   how many ounces of dough would make
   up each piece?

6. If the Most Pizzas Made in 1 Hour is 142,
   how many pizzas could be made at that rate
   in 2 1/2 hours? Explain your thinking.

MAKING A MASTERPIECE BY MOUTH

■ Check this out!

Largest Painting by Mouth

R. Rajendran (India) holds the Guinness World Records™ record for making the world's Largest Painting by Mouth! Rajendran created the record-setting painting over a 12-day period. Guinness judges measured the final painting in October 2007.

The artist named the painting *Mother Teresa Service to the World* to honor Mother Teresa, a world-famous nun. She was known for her work serving orphans and the poor throughout India.

The painting measures 30 feet long by 20 feet high. Rajendran started the painting as several smaller pieces of artwork. Then, he joined all of them together to create the final painting. This artist must have very strong mouth and tongue muscles!

MORE AMAZING RECORDS

Most Expensive Painting by Elephants: On February 19, 2005, 8 elephants in Thailand created a painting that sold for $39,000.

Most Non-Duplicated Fingerprints in 1 Artwork: The Foundation for the Defense of Our Values (Colombia) compiled 42,515 unique children's fingerprints on a single canvas.

World's Largest Popcorn Mosaic: To celebrate 10 years of popcorn in Russia, 9 Russian artists used popcorn to form a 1,076-square-foot mosaic in 2000.

Name_____ Date_____

■ Answer the questions. Show your work.

1. Rajendran's painting measures 9.14 meters long. In which place value is the 4?

   A. hundreds   **B.** tenths

   C. ones   **D.** hundredths

2. Rajendran's painting measures 20 feet high. It is _____ inches high.

3. The world's Largest Painting by Mouth measures 30 feet long by 20 feet high. What is the area of the painting?

   A. 50 feet   **B.** 100 square feet

   C. 600 square feet   **D.** 12,000 cubic feet

4. A group of 9 artists created a 1,076-square-foot mosaic made of popcorn. On **average**, how many square feet of the mosaic did each artist create? Round the answer to the nearest tenth.

5. Rajendran's painting measures 30 feet long by 20 feet high. What is the perimeter of the painting?

   A. 100 feet   **B.** 50 feet

   C. 10 feet   **D.** 40 feet

6. If Rajendran took 12 days to create a painting with an area of 55.75 square meters, what is the average number of square meters he painted each day? Round the answer to the nearest tenth.

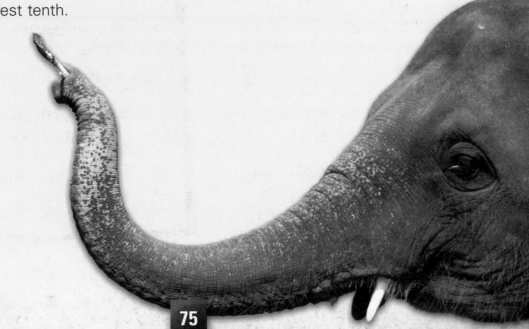

MAN VERSUS MACHINE

■ Check this out!

Longest Time Restraining 2 Aircraft

Is it a plane? Is it a strongman? Yes! It is Chad Netherland (USA). This strongman holds the world record for the Longest Time Restraining 2 Aircraft. To set the record, Netherland stopped the takeoff of 2 Cessna airplanes pulling in opposite directions, using only his own strength!

Netherland held 2 thick rubber bands. Each band attached to 1 of the airplanes. The strongman stood between the airplanes while stretching his arms out. By doing so, Netherland delayed the small airplanes' takeoffs for a total of 1 minute, 0.6 seconds. Netherland broke the record on July 7, 2007, at an airport in Superior, Wisconsin.

MORE AMAZING RECORDS

Longest Time Restraining a Car: Frank Muellner (Austria) restrained a Ferrari 360 Modena on full power for 13.84 seconds. The car has a top speed of 186 miles per hour.

Heaviest Train Pulled by Teeth: In 2003, Velu Rathakrishnan (Malaysia) used only his teeth to pull 2 commuter trains a distance of 13 feet 9 inches.

Heaviest Vehicle Pulled More Than 100 Feet— Male: Kevin Fast (Canada) set the record for the Heaviest Vehicle Pulled More Than 100 Feet by a Male. The vehicle weighed nearly 126,200 pounds. Fast set the record on live TV on September 15, 2008.

Name_____ Date_____

■ Answer the questions. Show your work.

1. When restraining the 2 airplanes, Netherland held his arms directly out from his sides. If his arms formed a straight line, his arms made a _____ degree angle.

2. Rathakrishnan pulled 2 commuter trains 13 feet 9 inches. How many inches did Rathakrishnan pull the trains?
    A. 22 inches
    B. 117 inches
    C. 156 inches
    D. 165 inches

3. Netherland restrained 2 airplanes for a total of 1 minute, 0.6 seconds. If he had restrained the airplanes for twice as long, he would have restrained them for _____ .

4. Fast pulled a vehicle weighing 126,200 pounds. How many ounces did the vehicle weigh?
    A. 63.1 ounces
    B. 7,887.5 ounces
    C. 2,019,200 ounces
    D. 252,400,000 ounces

5. Netherland broke the record for restraining 2 airplanes on July 7. On which day of the year, assuming it is not a leap year, did Netherland set the record?
    A. 180th
    B. 181st
    C. 184th
    D. 188th

THERE'S SOMETHING IN YOUR EAR!

■ Check this out!

Longest Ear Hair

For most people, the longest hair they have is on the head. What if your longest hair came from your ear? The world's Longest Ear Hair is more than 7 inches long! That is about as long as a pencil. The record-setting hair belongs to Anthony Victor (India). He used to be a school principal, and people called him "the ear-haired teacher."

Guinness World Records judges measured the hair growing from Victor's ear in 2007. They measured from the center of his outer ear to the tip of the longest strand.

Victor had broken the ear hair record once before. That was in 2002. At that time, his ear hair was about 4 1/2 inches long. Another man from India held the record until Victor broke it.

MORE AMAZING RECORDS

Farthest Ear Slingshot: In 2008, Monte Pierce (USA) used his ear as a slingshot. He shot a dime almost 12 feet!

Most Hair Donated to Charity in 24 Hours: In 2007, 881 people gave hair to charity. They gave 107 pounds of hair in 24 hours.

Longest Braid of Hair—Mass Participation: The Longest Braid of Hair was more than 123 feet! The braid was made in 1998 from the hair of 65 people.

Name_____ Date_____

■ Answer the questions. Show your work.

1. Which tool would be the best for measuring the length of Victor's ear hair?

   A. ruler

   B. meterstick

   C. tape measure

   D. yardstick

2. The _____ of the hair that was collected for charity was 48.72 kilograms.

   A. length

   B. weight

   C. height

   D. width

3. How long did it take for Victor's ear hair to grow from about 4 1/2 inches long to more than 7 inches long? Write a number sentence to explain your thinking.

4. In 2007, Victor's ear hair was about _____ inches longer than it was in 2002.

   A. $1\frac{1}{2}$

   B. $2\frac{1}{2}$

   C. 4

   D. $6\frac{1}{2}$

5. If you shot a dime 150 inches using your ear as a slingshot, would you break the world record?

6. Suppose a braid was made from the hair of 130 people, and each person's hair was about the same length as the hair that was used to break the record in 1998. About how long would the braid be?

   A. about 38 feet

   B. about 75 feet

   C. about 123 feet

   D. about 246 feet

A RECORD-SETTING ROBOT

■ Check this out!
Farthest Distance Covered by a Quadruped Robot

Contrary to its name, BigDog did not set a record for being the biggest dog. BigDog is a record-setting robot! Like a dog, BigDog moves on 4 legs. It set the Guinness World Records™ record by walking 12.7 miles. That is the farthest distance walked by a 4-legged robot! BigDog was designed to carry heavy loads over rough trails. It can balance itself through mud, snow, ice, and thick brush. It measures about 3 feet by 2 feet and weighs 165 pounds. Taking this BigDog for a walk could be quite a challenge!

BigDog image courtesy of Boston Dynamics ©2009

MORE AMAZING RECORDS

Fastest 2-Wheeled Robot: The Fastest 2-Wheeled Robot can move 3.7 miles per hour as set in March 2005.

Largest Robot Dog: The Largest Robot Dog measures 32 inches by 26 inches and can lift approximately 42 pounds.

Highest-Jumping Robot: The Highest-Jumping Robot can jump 30 feet in the air. This record was set in March 2001.

■ **Answer the questions. Show your work.**

1. Is the distance of 12.7 miles closer to 12 miles or 13 miles? Draw a number line to show your thinking.

2. To set the record, how far did BigDog walk in feet?

3. Which of the following weighs about the same as BigDog?
   - **A.** a small car
   - **B.** a small dog
   - **C.** a small man
   - **D.** a small fifth grader

4. If a fifth grader can jump 10.9 inches in the air, how much higher can the Highest-Jumping Robot jump?

5. Is BigDog larger or smaller than the Largest Robot Dog? Explain your thinking.

6. If BigDog moved at about the same rate as the Fastest 2-Wheeled Robot, estimate how many hours it would take for BigDog to travel its record-setting distance. Explain your thinking.

A MONSTER OF A TRUCK

■ Check this out!

Largest Monster Truck

Have you ever climbed into a car or truck using a very tall ladder? That's what you would have to do if you were going to ride in *Bigfoot #5*. That's the name of the world's Largest Monster Truck. *Bigfoot #5* is huge! It stands 15 feet 5 inches tall and weighs 38,000 pounds. Its tires are 10 feet tall—taller than the world's Tallest Person! Each tire weighs 2,400 pounds, which is heavier than the weight of a small car.

Bigfoot #5 is one of many Bigfoot trucks built by Bob Chandler (USA). The first was a pickup truck Chandler used for showing off the truck parts he sold in his shop. As he added new parts, his truck, which he named *Bigfoot #1*, kept getting bigger. It reached a weight of 11,000 pounds. At 10 feet 5 inches, it is just a shorty compared to *Bigfoot #5*!

MORE AMAZING RECORDS

Longest Ramp Jump: *Bigfoot #14* jumped 202 feet over a Boeing 727 passenger jet on September 11, 1999.

Fastest Speed: *Bigfoot #14* reached a speed of 69.3 miles per hour during the run-up to its Longest Ramp Jump.

Highest Ramp Jump: *Bigfoot #14* reached a height of 24 feet—more than twice its height—on December 14, 1999.

Name_____ Date_____

■ Answer the questions. Show your work.

1. How much taller and heavier is *Bigfoot #5* than *Bigfoot #1*?

2. What is the weight of 1 of *Bigfoot #5*'s tires in ounces?

3. How many tons does *Bigfoot #5* weigh?
   - **A.** 38 tons
   - **B.** 190 tons
   - **C.** 2,000 tons
   - **D.** 19 tons

4. The average height of a 10-year-old is about 56 inches. How many inches taller is 1 of *Bigfoot #5*'s tires than a 10-year-old?

5. *Bigfoot #14* jumped 24 feet high, which was more than twice its own height. If *Bigfoot #5* jumped twice its own height, how many feet higher than *Bigfoot #14* would it jump?

6. If 1 pickup truck weighs 6,800 pounds, and another weighs 8,800 pounds, how many would you need of each truck to equal the weight of *Bigfoot #5*?

THAT'S A LOT OF HAIR!

■ Check this out!

Longest Beard Dreadlock for a Living Male

How long do you think human hair can grow? What about facial hair? Shri Shri Baba Shri Ji of India might just find out. He holds the Guinness World Records™ record for the Longest Beard Dreadlock for a Living Male. When his beard was measured on November 23, 2008, it stretched 6 feet from the end of his chin to the tip of the beard. Imagine how many different ways you could style 6 feet of dreadlocks!

Dreadlocks form when the hair is intentionally matted and coiled to form long twisted sections of hair. As Shri Shri Baba Shri Ji shows, dreadlocks can be created from either scalp or beard hair.

MORE AMAZING RECORDS

Longest Moustache: Ram Singh Chauan (India) holds the record for the world's Longest Moustache. It stretched 14 feet when it was measured on March 4, 2010.

Longest Hair for a Female: As of May 8, 2004, the hair of Xie Qiuping (China) stretched 18 feet 5.5 inches. She has not cut her hair since 1973, when she was 13 years old.

Longest Beard for a Living Male: Sarwan Singh (Canada) holds the record for the Longest Beard for a Living Male. As of March 4, 2010, it measured 7 feet 9 inches.

Name_____ Date_____

■ **Answer the questions. Show your work.**

1. Shri Shri Baba Shri Ji's beard dreadlock is 6 feet long. That is equal to
   _____ yards.

2. If Shri Shri Baba Shri Ji's beard dreadlock grew to 1 1/4 of its current length, how long
   would it be in feet?

3. Calculate the age of Qiuping when she broke the world record for Longest Hair for
   a Female.

4. How many days remained in 2008 when Shri Shri Baba Shri Ji broke the record for
   the Longest Beard Dreadlock for a Living Male?

5. If Qiuping's hair continued to grow at the same rate, **about** how long would
   her hair be 5 years from the date she set the record?
   A. 20.5 feet
   B. 21.5 feet
   C. 31 feet
   D. 36 feet

6. Which of the following would be the best for finding the middle length of the
   hair of people in a beard-growing contest?
   A. mode
   B. range
   C. mean
   D. median

SAFETY FIRST?

■ Check this out!

Side-Wheel Driving (Can Scooping)

Safety comes first when driving. But, Sven-Erik Söderman (Sweden) ignores this rule as he swerves and zips from side to side across the track. Söderman holds the Guinness World Records™ record for Side-Wheel Driving, also known as Can Scooping. On September 12, 2001, Söderman scooped up 15 cans of food while driving his car on 2 wheels. Söderman had to grab the cans of food through his open car window while driving. The cans could not be side by side; the cans had to be set on opposite sides of a track that was at least 10 feet wide. So, Söderman had to zigzag across the track to scoop up the cans.

MORE AMAZING RECORDS

Earliest Flying Car: In 15 seconds, the Terrafugia *Transition*® changes from a car to an aircraft. It burns 5 gallons of fuel for 1 hour in the air and gets 30 miles per gallon on the road. The vehicle costs about $200,000!

Most Defensive Features on a Pickup Truck: The U.S. Army's *SmarTruck* boasts Kevlar® armor, bulletproof glass, electric door handles, and tire-piercing tacks. Its night vision video cameras can rotate 360 degrees.

Earliest Submarine Car: Rinspeed created the *sQuaba*, the world's Earliest Submarine Car. The car can drive directly into water. It travels underwater to a depth of up to 10 meters. Drivers must wear scuba gear while the car is underwater.

■ Answer the questions. Show your work.

1. Which would be the best unit to express the total weight of the cans collected by Söderman?

   A. gram

   B. meter

   C. pound

   D. liter

2. How many full circles can a video camera on the *SmarTruck* make in 1 rotation?

3. How many road miles would the Earliest Flying Car be able to drive on 6 gallons of fuel?

4. How many quarters are in $200,000?

5. How long could the Terrafugia *Transition*® fly on 23 gallons of fuel?

   A. 2 hours

   B. 4.6 hours

   C. 5 hours

   D. 7.5 hours

6. Estimate the length of the track that Söderman drove when breaking his record. Consider that he zigzagged across a 10-foot-wide track to pick up 15 cans. Explain your thinking.

WHAT'S THAT SMELL?

■ Check this out!

Smelliest Substance

Do you have a favorite smell? What about freshly baked bread, flowers, or the air at the beach? No matter what you enjoy smelling, you most likely would not like *Who-Me?* or *U.S. Government Standard Bathroom Malodor* because they stink! The 2 man-made substances are deemed to be the worst-smelling items in the world by Guinness World Records™. *Who-Me?* is made of 5 chemicals, while *U.S. Government Standard Bathroom Malodor* contains 8. The *Malodor* smells like human waste! It smells so bad that it repels humans at just 2 parts per million. While it smells horrible, the substance actually has a scientific use. It was designed to test how well cleaning products work at removing bad smells.

MORE AMAZING RECORDS

Most Feet and Armpits Sniffed: During her 15 years at a product testing lab, Madeline Albrecht (USA) smelled about 5,600 feet and an unknown number of armpits.

Smelliest Cheese: Vieux Boulogne, a soft French cheese, smelled worse than 14 other contenders in a 2004 contest sponsored by the Fine Cheese from France campaign. A group of 19 human judges and 1 electronic judge found that the cheese, described as a mix of farmyard smell and dung, could be smelled from a distance of 164 feet!

Name_____ Date_____

■ Answer the questions. Show your work.

1. Vieux Boulogne can be smelled from _____ yards away. Round the answer to the nearest whole number.

2. Which type of graph would best show the number of feet that Madeline Albrecht sniffed each year?
   A. stem-and-leaf plot
   B. line plot
   C. circle graph
   D. bar graph

3. Find the mean number of chemicals used in *Who-Me?* and *U.S. Government Standard Bathroom Malodor.*

4. Write as a percentage the amount of *U.S. Government Standard Bathroom Malodor* that repels humans.

5. Which description best represents the amount of *U.S. Government Standard Bathroom Malodor* that repels humans?
   A. 100 hundreds grids with 1 shaded individual square
   B. 100,000 hundreds grids with 2 shaded grids
   C. 1,000,000 hundreds grids with 2 shaded individual squares
   D. 10,000 hundreds grids with 2 shaded individual squares

6. Assuming that Madeline Albrecht smelled both feet and armpits of each person she tested, how many people did she smell during her career? Explain your thinking.

INTERESTING ALTERNATIVE ENERGY

■ Check this out!
Most Electricity Generated by Pedaling on Bikes for 24 Hours

Riding a bike provides great exercise. For this record, bikes were also used to create electricity. The Ender Werbung GmbH group (Austria) holds the Guinness World Records™ record for the Most Electricity Generated by Pedaling on Bikes for 24 Hours.

In April 2008, visitors to the Dornbirner Messe fair in Dornbirn, Austria, joined the group. To break the record, the group rode 21 bikes for 24 hours. Their pedaling created 12,953 watt hours of electricity!

Kilowatt hours measure how much electric power is used. One kilowatt hour equals 1,000 watts per hour.

MORE AMAZING RECORDS
Most Powerful Solar Power Tower: The PS10 power plant in Spain generates up to 11 megawatts of power. It uses 624 mirrors that are 120 square meters each. The mirrors focus light on the top of a 115-meter-high tower. The light drives an engine to produce electricity.

Most Powerful Tidal Power Station: The La Rance Tidal Barrage in France uses 24 engines powered by rising and falling tides. The engines create 240 megawatts of electricity, enough to power a city of 300,000 people.

Most Energy-Efficient Shoe: In 2000, Trevor Baylis (UK) and Texon International created a shoe that generates electricity. After walking 74.6 miles, Baylis made a phone call using power made by the shoe.

■ Answer the questions. Show your work.

1. What is the greatest common factor of 21 and 24?

2. On average, each bike generated _____ watt hours of electricity. Round the answer to the nearest hundredth.

3. Which would be the best unit to measure the electricity generated by Baylis's shoe?

    A. watt

    B. kilometer

    C. liter

    D. hour

4. Which equation would you use to determine how many megawatts of electricity would be needed to power a city of 750,000 people? (n represents the megawatts of electricity.)

    A. $(240)n = (300,000)(750,000)$

    B. $(750,000)n = (240)(300,000)$

    C. $(240)n = (300,000)(1,000)$

    D. $(300,000)n = (240)(750,000)$

5. Estimate how many total watt hours would have been generated at the fair if 5 more bikes had been ridden.

    A. 14,032 watt hours

    B. 16,016 watt hours

    C. 17,787 watt hours

    D. 20,000 watt hours

6. Assuming that power would have been generated at the same rate, how many watt hours of electricity would have been generated if the participants had pedaled for 36 hours? Explain your thinking.

A TALL ORDER

■ Check this out!
Tallest Living Married Couple

Wilco (Netherlands) and Keisha van Kleef-Bolton (UK) take the Guinness World Records™ record for being the Tallest Living Married Couple. The couple has a combined height of 13 feet 3.3 inches! Wilco is 6 feet 9.75 inches, and Keisha is 6 feet 5.5 inches tall.

How did these tall people meet? Keisha was looking for a dance partner. She contacted the United Kingdom's Tall Persons Club in hopes of finding just that. She ended up finding a dance partner and a husband all in one!

MORE AMAZING RECORDS

Tallest Living Man: What stands 8 feet 1 inch? The world's Tallest Living Man! Sultan Kosen (Turkey) holds this world record.

Tallest Girl: Malee Duangdee (Thailand) holds the Guinness World Records™ record for being the tallest female under the age of 18. She measured 6 feet 10 inches on January 16, 2009.

Tallest Boy: The world's tallest male under the age of 18 is Brenden Adams (USA). He is 7 feet 4.6 inches tall.

Name_____ Date_____

■ Answer the questions. Show your work.

1. What is the difference in height between the world's Tallest Boy and the world's Tallest Girl?

2. List the 5 tallest people from page 92 in order from shortest to tallest.

3. How much taller is Wilco than his wife, Keisha?

4. The average height of a fifth grader is 4 feet 8 inches tall. How much more would a fifth grader have to grow to reach the height of the world's Tallest Living Man?

5. If Wilco and Keisha's dance floor measures 25 feet by 20 feet, what is the total area of their dance floor?

6. Round the heights of the 5 tallest people to the nearest foot. Then, find the median.

BIG BUCKS

■ Check this out!

Most Expensive Bathroom

A jewelry shop owner in Hong Kong, China, decided to go all out on his shop's bathroom, spending his way to a Guinness World Records™ record for the Most Expensive Bathroom. Jeweler Lam Sai-wing spent $3.5 million on this one room! The toilets, sinks, mirror frames, chandeliers, wall tiles, and doors are made of solid, 24-carat gold. If that is not enough, the ceiling is covered in rubies, sapphires, emeralds, and amber, and the floor is covered with 2-pound gold bars.

MORE AMAZING RECORDS

Most Expensive Fungus Species: The world's Most Expensive Fungus Species is the white truffle. This rare fungus costs $3,000 for about 2 pounds!

Most Expensive Car: A classic 1963 Ferrari was sold for a whopping $17.275 million to Chris Evans (UK) in May 2010.

Most Expensive Computer Mouse: The world's Most Expensive Computer Mouse sells for $24,180! It is made of 18-carat white gold and is covered with 59 diamonds!

Name_____ Date_____

■ Answer the questions. Show your work.

1. About how much would it cost to buy 5 pounds of white truffle fungus?

2. How much more did the 1963 Ferrari cost than Sai-wing's bathroom?

3. How many ounces are the gold bars that cover the floor in the world's Most Expensive Bathroom?

4. If Sai-wing opened up 4 more jewelry stores and created the exact same bathroom for each store, what is the total amount he would have spent on all 5 bathrooms?

5. If each diamond on the world's Most Expensive Computer Mouse was worth $5,000, how much would the diamonds on the computer mouse be worth altogether?

6. If someone had 5 computers and bought the world's Most Expensive Computer Mouse for each computer, how much money would she spend in all?

AN EYEFUL

■ Check this out!
Farthest Milk Squirting Distance

On September 1, 2004, Ilker Yilmaz of Turkey set an eye-catching Guinness World Records™ record. He squirted milk farther than any other human. How he squirted the milk is the surprising part. He did not squirt milk from his mouth like you might think. Amazingly, he squirted the milk from his eye! To accomplish this, Yilmaz snorts milk up his nose, clamps his nose shut with his hand, and then squirts the milk out of his eye through his tear duct. He was able to squirt milk out of his eye a total of 9 feet 2 inches!

MORE AMAZING RECORDS
Fastest Time to Ignite 5 Targets by Squirting Milk from the Eye: Ilker Yilmaz (Turkey) holds the Guinness World Records™ record for igniting 5 targets using milk from his eye in just 1 minute, 44 seconds. A small amount of a special chemical in each glass allows the milk to light the targets on fire.

Fastest Time to Extinguish 5 Candles by Squirting Milk from the Eye: Ru Anting (China) took a mere 17 seconds to extinguish 5 candles by squirting milk out of his eye!

Most Vertical Water Squirts in 1 Minute: On June 18, 2009, Chen Chun of China hit a target 104 times in 1 minute. The target was almost 10 feet above him!

Name_____ Date_____

■ Answer the questions. Show your work.

1. How many total inches was Yilmaz able to squirt milk from his eye?

2. If Yilmaz was trying to ignite a candle 105 inches away, would he be able to squirt that far according to his world record? Explain your thinking.

3. If Anting was able to keep his pace of extinguishing 5 candles every 17 seconds, how long would it take him to extinguish 25 candles?

4. If Yilmaz was also able to keep his pace of igniting 5 targets in 1 minute, 44 seconds, how long would it take him to ignite 15 targets?

5. Estimate how many seconds it took Yilmaz to ignite each of the 5 candles. Explain your thinking.

6. Estimate how many seconds it took Anting to extinguish 1 of his 5 candles. Explain your thinking.

GIDDYUP!

■ Check this out!

Largest Horseshoe

Blacksmithing is a trade long practiced in history. Using special tools and extreme heat, craftsmen forge metal into various items. At the 2008 International Blacksmith Festival in Austria, 8 people broke a Guinness World Records™ record by creating the Largest Horseshoe. To create this record-setting horseshoe, the team began with a piece of flat steel measuring 2 inches tall, 1 inch wide, and 4 feet 5 inches long. Once complete, the horseshoe measured 1 foot 10 inches tall and 2 feet wide.

MORE AMAZING RECORDS

Largest Cowbell: Venter-Glocken (Germany) created a cowbell weighing more than 1 ton! The Largest Cowbell is 10 feet 9 inches tall and weighs a hefty 2,028 pounds.

Largest Horseshoe Sculpture: Donnie Faulk (USA) used 1,071 horseshoes to create the world's Largest Horseshoe Sculpture. The sculpture is a life-size horse.

Largest Cowboy Boot: The world's Largest Cowboy Boot is 8 feet 2 inches tall and 7 feet 10 inches long. It was made in Ethiopia. Imagine the cowboy who would wear it!

Name_____ Date_____

■ **Answer the questions. Show your work.**

1. Round the height of the world's Largest Cowbell to the nearest foot.

2. The world's Largest Cowbell weighs about 1 _____ .
   A. pound   B. ton
   C. gallon   D. foot

3. If Faulk decided to create more horse sculptures using the same number of horseshoes for each sculpture, how many horseshoes would he need to create a family of 4?

4. How much taller is the world's Largest Cowbell than the world's Largest Horseshoe?

5. Imagine that 15 giant cows needed cowbells. If they were each able to wear 1 cowbell weighing the same as the world's Largest Cowbell, how many total pounds of cowbells would there be?

6. The average length of fifth grader's foot is 8 inches. Estimate how many fifth-grade feet would be needed to equal the length of the world's Largest Cowboy Boot.

HELLO?

■ Check this out!

Toughest Mobile Phone

The JCB TOUGHPHONE is just that—tough. The TOUGHPHONE takes the Guinness World Records™ record for being the world's Toughest Mobile Phone. What makes this phone so tough? When Guinness World Records judges dropped the phone from a height of 10 feet 8 inches onto concrete, it did not even get a scratch. And, it worked right after the drop!

Not only can the TOUGHPHONE survive great falls, but it is also completely water-resistant. If that is not enough to earn the title of world's Toughest Mobile Phone, this last fact seals the deal: the TOUGHPHONE can withstand the weight of a large vehicle driving over it without getting damaged!

MORE AMAZING RECORDS

Earliest Dog to Detect Cell Phones: Murphy, a springer spaniel, was trained to sniff out cell phones! Murphy was just 15 months old when he started working in September 2006. The Eastern Area Drug Dog team (UK) trained him.

Largest Telephone: A crane is needed to use this telephone! The world's Largest Telephone is 8 feet 1 inch tall, 19 feet 11 inches long, and it weighs 3 1/2 tons.

Most Telephone Books Ripped in 2 Minutes: In March 2010, Cosimo Ferrucci (Italy) ripped 32 telephone books with his hands in 2 minutes! Each phone book had 1,007 pages.

Name_____ Date_____

■ Answer the questions. Show your work.

1. From a height of how many total inches could the JCB TOUGHPHONE be dropped and survive the fall?

2. Could the TOUGHPHONE be dropped from the top of the world's Largest Telephone and survive? Explain your thinking.

3. One ton equals 2,000 pounds. How many pounds does the world's Largest Telephone weigh?

4. Do you think the TOUGHPHONE could be dropped from a three-story building and not be damaged? Explain your thinking.

5. How many total phone book pages did Ferrucci rip through in 2 minutes?

6. If Ferrucci kept ripping at the same rate, how many phone books would he have ripped through in 8 minutes? Draw a table to show your answer.

COCONUTS GALORE

■ Check this out!

Fastest Time to Husk a Coconut

Husking a coconut requires skill and strength. Before opening the shell, the coarse, hair-like husk must first be removed. Then, a rock, stick, or knife can be used to pierce the coconut shell along 1 of the 3 seams.

Sidaraju Raju (India) holds the Guinness World Records™ record for the Fastest Time to Husk a Coconut. He managed to remove the shell in 28.06 seconds. He even used his teeth to succeed at this feat! Raju's coconut had a circumference of 30.7 inches, and it weighed 10 pounds 7.3 ounces. He set the record on March 30, 2003, in Bangalore, India.

MORE AMAZING RECORDS

Fastest Coconut Tree Climb: Fuatai Solo (Fiji) climbed a coconut tree 29 feet 6 inches tall in 4.88 seconds! At that rate, Solo could have climbed the Empire State Building in about 4 minutes! Solo set the record in August 1980.

Most Coconuts Pierced with 1 Finger in 30 Seconds: Ho Eng Hui (Malaysia) pierced 4 coconuts with his index finger in only 30 seconds. Hui set the record in June 2009.

Most Coconuts Smashed in 1 Minute with 1 Hand: Muhamed Kahrimanovic (Germany) smashed 82 coconuts in 1 minute by only using 1 hand. He broke the record in Vienna, Austria, in September 2009.

Name_____ Date_____

■ Answer the questions. Show your work.

1. What does circumference express?
   - **A.** the inside volume of a sphere
   - **B.** the distance around a circle or sphere
   - **C.** the inside volume of a trapezoid
   - **D.** the distance around a prism

2. Which type of graph would be the best for finding the median size of the coconuts used in a coconut competition?
   - **A.** line graph
   - **B.** pie chart
   - **C.** stem-and-leaf plot
   - **D.** bar graph

3. What was the weight of the coconut Raju husked in ounces?

4. If Ho Eng Hui continued piercing coconuts at the same rate, he could have pierced

   _____ coconuts in 2 1/2 minutes.

5. Write an equation that shows how to calculate the rate in seconds at which Kahrimanovic smashed the coconuts. Round the answer to the nearest hundredth.

6. Based on Solo's coconut tree climb, estimate the height of the Empire State Building in feet. Explain your thinking.

SENSATIONAL SOCCER

■ Check this out!
Farthest Distance Traveled with a Soccer Ball Balanced on the Head

Soccer is one of the most popular sports in the world. Soccer balls are not only used to score goals but also to break world records! Yee Ming Low (Malaysia) holds the Guinness World Records™ record for the Farthest Distance Traveled with a Soccer Ball Balanced on the Head. To set the record, Low walked 6.915 miles. It took him 2 hours, 38 minutes, 44 seconds to achieve the feat. He set the record on August 21, 2009, in Selangor, Malaysia.

MORE AMAZING RECORDS

Fastest Soccer Ball Kick: Francisco Javier Galan Màrin (Spain) kicked a soccer ball at a speed of 80.2 miles per hour. He broke the record on October 29, 2001.

Fastest Marathon Juggling a Soccer Ball: Jan Skorkovsky of Prague, Czech Republic, juggled a soccer ball without allowing it to hit the ground while traveling for 26.219 miles. It took him 7 hours, 18 minutes, 55 seconds to complete the feat.

Largest Collection of Soccer Balls: Roberto Fuglini (Argentina) owns 861 soccer balls. He began collecting them in 1995 after his previous collection, dating back to 1965, was destroyed in a fire.

Name_____ Date_____

■ Answer the questions. Show your work.

1. Fuglini began his first soccer ball collection in 1965. When the collection was destroyed in 1995, it was _____ years old.

2. Yee Ming Low balanced a soccer ball on his head for _____ feet.

3. From 1995 to 2010 when he set his record, Fuglini collected about _____ soccer balls per year.

4. Which formula would you use to determine the area of a soccer field? (l = length, w = width, b = base, h = height)

   A. l + w

   B. 2l + 2w

   C. l x w

   D. $\frac{1}{2}$ (b + h)

5. About how fast did Yee Ming Low walk to set the record?
   A. 2.8 miles per hour
   B. 3.5 miles per hour
   C. 5.0 miles per hour
   D. 6.9 miles per hour

6. Compare the rate at which Yee Ming Low walked to the rate at which Skorkovsky walked to set his record. Which man walked faster? Explain your thinking.

THE BOYS OF SUMMER

■ Check this out!

Most Baseballs Held in 1 Baseball Glove

The crack of the bat and the seventh-inning stretch mean baseball season! Watching a baseball game marks a pastime in many towns. In that spirit, some people even try to break Guinness World Records™ records about the sport itself.

Ashrita Furman (USA) held 22 baseballs in 1 baseball glove! That is a lot of weight to balance! He set the record on December 26, 2008, in Jamaica, New York.

Since 1979, Furman has broken 259 Guinness World Records™ records. He broke his first record by doing more than 27,000 jumping jacks. Furman even holds the record for breaking the most world records. He currently holds 100!

MORE AMAZING RECORDS

Oldest Baseball Field: Fuller Field in Clinton, Massachusetts, has hosted games since 1878.

Largest Baseball: The world's Largest Baseball was displayed at John Hancock All-Star FanFest in Pennsylvania in July 2006. It measured 12 feet in diameter and was signed by players Ted Williams and Hank Aaron.

Largest Wooden Baseball Bat: The record-setting baseball bat measures 161 inches long and has a circumference of 40 inches. The Fargo-Moorhead RedHawks baseball club of Fargo, North Dakota, owns the bat.

Most Expensive Baseball Glove: The glove from Lou Gehrig's (USA) final game in 1939 sold for $389,500. It sold at auction in 1999.

Name_____ Date_____

■ **Answer the questions. Show your work.**

1. Fuller Field has hosted baseball games for _____ years.

2. Write the record number of jumping jacks completed by Furman in expanded form.

3. Furman broke about _____ records per year between 1979 and 2010.

4. What is the radius of the world's Largest Wooden Baseball Bat?
   - **A.** 6.4 inches
   - **B.** 12.8 inches
   - **C.** 31.4 inches
   - **D.** 62.8 inches

5. How many days elapsed between Gehrig's last game and the day his glove sold at the auction? Do not include leap years in your answer. Explain your thinking.

6. About how much larger is the diameter of the world's Largest Baseball than the diameter of the world's Largest Wooden Baseball Bat?
   - **A.** 161 inches
   - **B.** 144 inches
   - **C.** 131.2 inches
   - **D.** 12.7 inches

SUPERHUMAN STRENGTH

■ Check this out!

Most Arm Curl Weight in 1 Hour (Individual)

1, 2, 3, lift! The human body can do amazing things. Some physical feats, though, may seem impossible to achieve. But, Eamonn Keane (Ireland) holds the Guinness World Records™ record for lifting the Most Arm Curl Weight in 1 Hour. In 60 minutes, he lifted 51,324.8 pounds! To do so, Keane lifted a 48.4-pound dumbbell 1,058 times. He set the record on October 5, 2007. The record was witnessed by 3 members of the Powerhouse Gym in Dublin, Ireland. Imagine how Keane's arms felt after setting the record!

MORE AMAZING RECORDS

Heaviest Weight Lifted in a 24-Hour Bench Press by a Team of 9: A team of 9 bench-pressed a total of 11,063,237 pounds! The team set the record in February 2002 at Fitness First health club in Berkhamsted, United Kingdom. They set the record in just 19 hours.

Greatest Weight of Bricks Lifted: Fred Burton (UK) lifted and held 20 bricks at chest height for 2 seconds in 1998. The bricks weighed 226 pounds 8 ounces!

Most Flips of a 25-kilogram Weight in 1 Minute: Johnny Lindström (Sweden) flipped 55 pounds 1.84 ounces with 1 hand for a total of 24 times in 1 minute. He set the record in Stockholm, Sweden, on November 24, 2001.

Name_____ Date_____

■ Answer the questions. Show your work.

1. Which geometric figure does a brick most resemble?
    A. cylinder
    B. square pyramid
    C. rectangular prism
    D. sphere

2. Keane lifted a total of _____ ounces.

3. The weight lifted by Lindström is about _____ pounds more than the dumbbell lifted by Keane.

4. What is the total weight in pounds of 7 of the bricks lifted by Burton? Round the answer to the nearest hundredth.

5. Which equation best expresses the average weight in pounds lifted by 4 members of the 9-man team that lifted the heaviest weight in a 24-hour time period? (n represents the average weight.)
    A. $4n = (11{,}063{,}237/9)$
    B. $(11{,}063{,}237/9)(4) = n$
    C. $(9)(4) = (11{,}063{,}237)n$
    D. $(11{,}063{,}237/4) = 9n$

6. At what rate per second did Lindström flip his weight?

JOLLY JUGGLERS

■ Check this out!

Most Consecutive Foot-Juggling Flips

Have you ever tried to juggle? It takes focus and coordination, especially when it is done with the feet! Foot juggling involves juggling with the feet. Foot jugglers frequently work in pairs or groups to juggle balls or other objects between them—even people!

Hou Yanan and Jiang Tiantian (both China) hold the Guinness World Records™ record for the Most Consecutive Foot-Juggling Flips. They managed to foot juggle 90 times. They set the record on September 19, 2007, in Beijing, China. Yanan and Tiantian are members of the Wuqiao County Aerobatic Group.

MORE AMAZING RECORDS

Most Juggling Catches of 3 Objects While Suspended: Ashrita Furman (USA) completed 781 juggling ball catches while hanging upside down on November 21, 2009. Furman juggled for 5 minutes, 26.63 seconds.

Most Juggling Plate Catches Using 1 Hand: Francisco Tebar (Spain) juggled 5 plates 16 times with 1 hand. He broke the record in 2009.

Fastest Mile Juggling 3 Objects While Running in a Relay—Female: Sandy Brown, Kay Caskey, Kathy Glynn, and Laurie Young (USA) ran a 1-mile relay in 6 minutes, 54.1 seconds while each juggling 3 objects. They set the record in 1990 at the Joggling Championships in Los Angeles, California. Juggling while jogging is known as *joggling*.

Name_____ Date_____

■ Answer the questions. Show your work.

1. Brown, Caskey, Glynn, and Young ran _____ feet to set the record for Fastest Mile Juggling 3 Objects While Running in a Relay.

2. How many times each did Yanan and Tiantian foot juggle?

3. Brown, Caskey, Glynn, and Young joggled _____ seconds longer than Furman juggled ball catches while suspended upside down.

4. Write the prime factorization of the number of times that Yanan and Tiantian foot juggled.

5. Which explanation best expresses how to determine the total circumference of all of the plates juggled by Tebar?
   A. Square the length of the radius. Then, multiply it by 5 and pi (∏).
   B. Multiply the radius by 2 and pi (∏). Then, divide the product by 5.
   C. Square the length of the radius and multiply it by pi (∏). Divide the product by 5.
   D. Multiply the radius by 2 and pi (∏). Multiply that product by 5.

6. Which measure of central tendency would most accurately show the most number of times that Yanan and Tiantian foot juggled? Explain your thinking.

   mean   **mode**   **median**

HIGH JUMPERS

■ Check this out!

Most Vaults in 1 Hour

Do you like to jump? Do you think it is fun to fly through the air? Then, you might want to join the Blue Falcons Gymnastic Display Team in the United Kingdom. They perform many amazing stunts. Team members have even vaulted through hoops of fire and jumped over the length of a minibus. The team performs to raise money for charity.

On September 5, 2009, 10 members of the team broke the record for most vaults in 1 hour. The 14- to 18-year-old students vaulted a total of 6,250 times in Chelmsford, Essex, United Kingdom. The team formed in 1974 and has about 80 members. During shows, they perform for crowds with as many as 10,000 people!

MORE AMAZING RECORDS

Most Cars Hurdled in 1 Hour: In 1 hour in 1989, Jeff Clay (USA) jumped over 101 cars. He set the record in Fort Oglethorpe, Georgia.

Highest Pole Vault—Female: Yelena Isinbayeva (Russia) jumped 16 feet 7 inches. She set the record in 2009 in Zurich, Switzerland.

Fastest 10 Meters Frog Jumping: In 2007, Ashrita Furman (USA) frog jumped 32 feet 9.7 inches in 8.22 seconds. Frog jumping is jumping while holding on to your toes. Furman set the record in Jamaica, New York.

Highest High Jump—Male: Javier Sotomayor (Cuba) jumped 8 feet 0.46 inches in 1993. He set the record in Salamanca, Spain.

Name_____ Date_____

■ Answer the questions. Show your work.

1. Which would be the best unit for measuring the height jumped by Clay?
   - **A.** inch
   - **B.** foot
   - **C.** yard
   - **D.** mile

2. The Blue Falcons Gymnastic Display Team formed _____ years ago as of 2010.

3. Find the average number of times vaulted per minute by the Blue Falcons Gymnastic Display Team. Round to the nearest whole number.

4. Furman frog-jumped about _____ feet for every 1 foot jumped by Sotomayor.

5. What formula would you use to find the total area covered by Isinbayeva during her record-setting pole vault? Draw a picture to explain your thinking. (Hint: The pole vaulter ascends and descends at an angle. The 2 angles and the lateral area form a triangle.)

UNDERWATER WONDER

■ Check this out!

Deepest Cycling Underwater

Vittorio Innocente (Italy) created a new sport when he merged his hobbies of scuba diving and cycling. Imagine putting on scuba gear, hopping on a bike, and taking a ride in the water. Imagine being 218 feet 2 inches deep while doing so! Innocente did just that on July 21, 2008. He earned a Guinness World Records™ record for Deepest Cycling Underwater. He pedaled along a 361-foot underwater slope, dodging obstacles along the way, to reach the record depth. Innocente broke his old record of 197 feet set 3 years earlier.

MORE AMAZING RECORDS

Largest Underwater Golf Tournament: In 2007, a group of 5 players competed in the Largest Underwater Golf Tournament. The tournament was held in a 49-foot deepwater tank in China.

Largest Underwater Dance Class: A group of 74 students and teachers danced for 13 minutes, 30 seconds in the world's Largest Underwater Dance Class in Sydney, Australia, on October 27, 2006.

Largest Underwater Hockey Tournament: From September 2–6, 2009, in New Zealand, 62 different teams played in the world's Largest Underwater Hockey Tournament. A total of 564 players competed!

Name_____ Date_____

■ Answer the questions. Show your work.

1. In what year did Innocente set the record for cycling at a depth of 197 feet?

2. What is the difference in depth between the golfers' underwater golf tournament and Innocente's underwater cycling?

3. On July 21, 2008, Innocente broke his earlier record by about how many yards?

4. Innocente was cycling about _____ yards underwater.

5. If each of the 62 hockey teams only played once in the hockey tournament, how many total games were played?

6. Estimate how many players were on each of the hockey teams that participated in the Largest Underwater Hockey Tournament. Explain your thinking.

BALL PRO

■ Check this out!

Most Basketball Headers While Spinning 2 Basketballs

Basketball freestyler Tommy Baker (UK) knows how to dribble, bounce, juggle, and spin multiple basketballs at the same time. On February 16, 2009, he combined 2 of these skills to set a Guinness World Records™ record. Baker holds the record for Most Basketball Headers While Spinning 2 Basketballs.

A header is when someone bounces the ball off of his head. Baker was able to keep 1 ball spinning with his right hand and 1 ball spinning with his left hand while bouncing yet another ball 40 times on his head—all without dropping any of the 3 balls!

MORE AMAZING RECORDS

Longest Time Spinning a Basketball on the Nose: Scooter Christensen (USA) spun a basketball on his nose for 5.1 seconds in February 2010.

Longest Time Spinning a Basketball on 1 Toe: In February 2008, Jack Ryan (USA) spun a basketball on his toe for 9.53 seconds.

Longest Time to Spin a Basketball on 1 Finger: Joseph Odhiambo (USA) was able to spin a basketball on 1 finger using only 1 hand for 1 minute, 54.88 seconds in February 2009.

Name_____ Date_____

■ Answer the questions. Show your work.

1. Ryan spun a basketball on his toe for _____ seconds longer than Christensen spun a basketball on his nose.

2. If Baker were able to triple his record, how many times would he have headed the ball while spinning 2 basketballs?

3. Odhiambo was _____ seconds short of spinning a basketball on 1 finger for 2 minutes.

4. List the 4 Guinness World Records™ basketball events in chronological order.

5. How many seconds was Odhiambo able to keep a basketball spinning on 1 finger?

6. If the numbers below were Baker's practice scores for headers while spinning 2 basketballs, which score would be the median?

40, 38, 35, 40, 39, 21, 40

IT'S HAIR-RAISING!

■ Check this out!

Farthest Distance to Pull a Bus with the Hair

On November 11, 2009, Manjit Singh (UK) broke an amazing Guinness World Records™ record. Singh pulled a bus for 69 1/2 feet in a hair-raising way. He used his hair to pull the bus! The bus was not an ordinary bus either; it was a double-decker bus! A double-decker bus has 2 levels, so it is twice as tall as a regular bus. Singh pulled the double-decker bus using only a clamp attached to his ponytail.

Singh holds several Guinness World Records™ records, all involving strength and stamina. He enjoys setting records and uses his hobby to raise money for charity.

MORE AMAZING RECORDS

Most Llamas Pulling a Carriage: On September 1, 1997, Floyd Zopfi (USA) drove 64 llamas and 8 ponies together. He used reins 299 feet long!

Heaviest Vehicle Pulled by Rice Bowl Suction on the Stomach: Zhang Xingquan of China pressed a rice bowl to his stomach, creating enough suction to pull a 7,287-pound vehicle more than 32 feet!

Heaviest Train Pulled with a Beard: Ismael Rivas Falcon (Spain) pulled a 6,070-pound train for more than 32 feet—with his beard!

■ **Answer the questions. Show your work.**

1. Write the train's weight in word form.

2. About how much farther did Singh pull his vehicle than Falcon?

3. The vehicle Xingquan pulled weighed more than the train Falcon pulled. How much more did it weigh?

4. About how many inches was Xingquan able to pull the vehicle?

5. Singh pulled the double-decker bus 69 1/2 feet. Write this number as a decimal.

6. If Singh raised $1,000 for every 5 feet he moved the double-decker bus, about how much total money did he raise?

CRUSHED

■ Check this out!

Most Concrete Blocks Broken with the Elbow While Holding a Raw Egg

Joe Alexander of Germany has an extraordinarily strong arm and a surprisingly steady hand. It took a combination of these to set his Guinness World Records™ record for Most Concrete Blocks Broken with the Elbow While Holding a Raw Egg. On November 11, 2009, Alexander used his elbow to hit concrete blocks stacked on top of each other. He was able to break 11 concrete blocks with just a single hit! While breaking the blocks, he used the hand on the same arm to hold a raw egg—without cracking the egg!

MORE AMAZING RECORDS

Heaviest Concrete Block Break on a Bed of Nails: While laying on a bed of nails, Neal Hardy (Australia) had 16 blocks stacked on top of him. The concrete blocks were then broken while still on Hardy's chest! The 16 blocks weighed a total of 1,173 pounds.

Most Military Bench Press Lifts—Female: Virpi Nevala (Finland) lifted 121 pounds 47 times on August 17, 2002.

Name_____ Date_____

■ Answer the questions. Show your work.

1. The total weight of Hardy's 16 blocks was 1,173 pounds. Write the weight in expanded form.

2. If November 1, 2009, were a Sunday, what day did Alexander achieve his world record?

3. Nevala lifted 121 pounds 47 times without stopping. What is the total amount of weight that she lifted during that time?

4. How many times would Nevala have to lift 121 pounds to lift more than the weight stacked on top of Hardy?

5. Estimate the weight of one of the concrete blocks that was stacked on top of Hardy.

6. If the concrete blocks that Alexander and Hardy used were the same weight, what is the total weight of concrete blocks that Alexander broke through? Round the answer to the nearest whole number.

CHECKMATE

■ Check this out!
Largest Board Game Tournament

A total of 1,214 people played their way into the Guinness World Records™ record book on June 2, 2007. They participated in the world's Largest Board Game Tournament.

The gamers battled each other in chess. Chess is a popular board game for 2 players. Each player maneuvers 16 pieces around the checkered board trying to capture the other player's king.

The tournament took place in the city park in Krasnoyarsk, Russia. The event was organized by the city administration, education department, children's education center, and Public Limited Company.

MORE AMAZING RECORDS

Largest Collection of Board Games: Brian Arnett (USA) has been collecting board games since 1996. As of February 21, 2007, Brian had 1,345 different board games in his collection. It took Brian 3 weeks to carry all of his board games up from his basement!

Longest Marathon Playing a Board Game: In January 2009, 6 Canadians played *Catan: Cities & Knights* for 50 hours!

Largest Board Game of Fox and Hen: In 2006, Peter Zettel (Austria) created the Largest Board Game of Fox and Hen. He set the world record with a game board that was 20 feet 6 inches square.

■ Answer the questions. Show your work.

1. Number the records in chronological order.

    _____ Largest Board Game Tournament

    _____ Largest Collection of Board Games

    _____ Longest Marathon Playing a Board Game

    _____ Largest Board Game of Fox and Hen

2. How many participants were in the world's Largest Board Game Tournament? Write this number in word form.

3. Chess is a board game for 2 people. How many total board games could have been going on at the same time during the tournament on June 2, 2007?

4. Estimate the total area of the Fox and Hen game board. Draw a picture to show your thinking.

    A. 74 square feet

    B. 80 square feet

    C. 400 square feet

    D. 8,000 square feet

5. On average, how many board games was Arnett able to carry upstairs per day?

6. From 1996 to 2007, estimate how many board games Arnett collected each year. Explain your thinking.

DICE IT UP!

■ Check this out!

Largest Collection of Dice

Kevin Cook (USA) has a "dicey" hobby. He is a collector of dice! Cook started collecting dice in 1977. His collection broke the Guinness World Records™ record for being the Largest Collection of Dice in the world. How many dice does it take to break this world record? The official count of Cook's collection in 2004 was 11,097.

Cook's massive collection includes the common, 6-sided numbered dice in the shape of a cube. But, his collection also houses a variety of other dice. Some of his dice have 4, 12, or 20 sides; some of his dice have symbols, words, or letters instead of numbers; and some of his dice are made of glass, wood, or even paper!

MORE AMAZING RECORDS

Tallest Column of Dice: Hu Hai Rong of China constructed the world's Tallest Column of Dice on November 14, 2008. He used 25 dice to create his column.

Tallest Double Column of Dice: Hu Hai Rong also holds the Guinness World Records™ record for creating the Tallest Double Column of Dice. He used 42 dice to set this record.

Name_____ Date_____

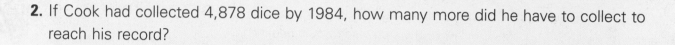

1. Cook collected _____ dice to break the record for world's Largest Collection of Dice. Write the answer in expanded form.

2. If Cook had collected 4,878 dice by 1984, how many more did he have to collect to reach his record?

3. At the time he broke the record, how many years had Cook been collecting dice?

4. How many more dice were used in Hu Hai Rong's double column than in his single column of dice?

5. How many record-breaking single columns of dice could Hu Hai Rong construct with Cook's dice collection?

6. How many record-breaking double columns of dice could Hu Hai Rong construct with Cook's dice collection?

ANSWER KEY

Page 11

1. 8; 2. 1 foot 9 inches; 3. taller; 3/4 of a yard is 27 inches; an Old English mastiff grows up to 32 inches tall; 4. C.; 5. 20; 6. 191, 192, 194

Page 13

1. equal to; 2. 220; 3. 7.8 inches; 4. 1,100 pounds; 5. B.; 6. 1/8

Page 15

1. 10.6 miles per hour; 2. 18 feet 1 inch; 3. B, D, C, A; 4. 1962 – Suggested answers: a) Subtract 2 from 1914 to get the year of the alligator's birth (1912). Then, add 50 to get 1962. b) In 1978, the alligator was 66. Subtract 16 from 1978 to get the year it was 50; 5. 1,000 pounds and 1,050 pounds – Suggested answer: Crocodiles weigh about 1,000 pounds, and 1,000 + 1,050 = 2,050.

Page 17

1. 12.6; Students' drawings should include a number line labeled 12.50 and 12.60 and divided into 10 units between 12.50 to 12.60 with a bold dot at 12.59; 2. 394 inches; 3. 14.09 seconds; 4. 65 feet 8 inches; 5. 16.3 meters per second; 6. less than 1/4 minute; Suggested answer: 1/4 minute is 15 seconds, and Warhol's time was 12.59 seconds.

Page 19

1. C.; 2. circumference of the Largest Duck Egg; 3. less than; 4. 200 eggs. Suggested answer: Each egg is 0.5 pounds, and 0.5 × 200 = 100; 5. 1 2/3 feet; 20 inches; 6. 6 times

Page 21

1. D.; 2. 5,000; 3. 1,980,000; 4. 2,005,000; 5. 4 – Suggested answer: Each penguin is 2 1/4 feet, so 4 are needed to make 9 feet.; 6. 10 – Suggested answer: Add the numbers in the pattern (1 + 2 + 3 . . .) until a sum of 55 is reached. Then, look for the last number in the pattern.

Page 23

1. 2.3 inches; 2. 2 2/5 inches, 3/10 ounces; 3. $29.25; 4. 400 yards; 5. 876,000 days; 6. about 50

Page 25

1. C.; 2. 406; 3. 11 feet 3.33 inches; 4. 2 feet 4 inches; 5. B.; 6. about 0.005 or 1/200 of a mile – Suggested answer: Round amounts to 25 feet/5,000 feet per mile.

Page 27

1. 0.23 seconds; 2. B. – Suggested answer: The stopwatch would depend on a person to stop and start it, and a person could not react quickly enough. The naked eye can only observe, not measure, time. A high-speed camera could capture the event and be used to measure the time. A thermometer measures temperature, not time; 3. 0.21, 21/100; 4. 1.5 grams; 5. 5h = 25,000; h = 25,000/5; h = 5,000; 6. About 5 1/2 – Suggested answer: Divide the human reaction time of 650 milliseconds by the mole reaction time of 120 milliseconds (650 ÷ 120 = 5.4).

Page 29

1. 25 ounces; 2. 25/26; 3. 33; 4. 6 minutes, 9 minutes, 12 minutes; 5. 90 degrees; 6. 100 meters is longer. – Suggested answer: 1 yard equals 36 inches, and 1 meter equals about 39 inches. 100 yards would equal about 360 inches, and 100 meters would equal about 390 inches.

Page 31

1. foot; 2. 6 years; 3. 230 pounds; 4. 12 square feet; 5. 21; 6. about 3

Page 33

1. fish egg, dinosaur egg, duck egg; 2. five and five-tenths; 3. C.; 4. 12; 5. 14 cups; 6. 20,000 pounds

Page 35

1. 10 + 9 + 0.7; 2. 400,000; 3. 27 years; 4. C.; 5. about 90 yards; 6. 1,320,000 tons

Page 37

1. 1/2 meter; 2. 350 centimeters; 3. 200 yards; 4. 2,928 hours; 5. 2 explosions – Suggested answer: With 6 explosions, there is 1 every 10 minutes; after 20 minutes, there would be 2 explosions; 6. One possibility is 50 miles and 22.06 miles. Because you need to multiply the length and width of a rectangle to get the area, you need two numbers (that are not equal) whose product is 1,103.

Page 39

1. 2 tenths; 2. 4 inches; 3. 10.24 ounces; 4. A.; 5. 181.75 inches; 6. 15 seconds – Suggested answer: 4 peppers is 1/4 of the 16; 1/4 of 60 seconds (1 minute) is 15 seconds.

Page 41

1. C.; 2. 18.46 Earth days; 3. 53,515 miles; 4. 4.48 billion kilometers; 5. about 8 months; 6. shorter – Suggested answer: 2 days on Jupiter equals about 19 hours, 50 minutes, which is shorter than Earth's 24-hour day.

Page 43

1. A.; 2. 8 feet 6 inches; 3. 6,500 tons; 4. about 2,802; 5. 150 days; 6. 41

Page 45

1. C.; 2. 1,500 feet ÷ 3 = 1,500 meters; 3. B.; 4. 21,529,922 square feet; 5. C.

Page 47

1. C.; 2. 252.9 pounds; 3. 4,046.4 ounces; 4. 3,448 ounces; 5. 113.8 pounds

Page 49

1. $1,200,000,000; 2. C.; 3. $1 billion; 4. 15 feet 9 inches; 5. about 35; 6. C. – Suggested answer: A bar graph allows a different bar to represent each storm and the damage it caused. A line graph shows change over time, a pie chart shows percentages of a whole, and a stem-and-leaf plot shows specific numerical data of one item.

Page 51

1. 7,000 feet; 2. 21 years; 3. 5 ounces; 4. 36 inches; 5. about 65 yards; 6. 21 feet

Page 53

1. 0.4 kilometers; 2. 10,000 + 6,000 + 800 + 30; 3. July 1975; 4. about $1.10 per pound; 5. C.; 6. about 36 inches

Page 55

1. one thousand three hundred fifteen; 2. C.; 3. 28 days; 4. 600 pounds; 5. 1,315 pounds × 3 = 3,945 pounds; 6. 692 pounds

Page 57

1. 74 minutes; 2. 30; 3. 8; 4. 199 months; 5. 1 hour, 1 minute, 44 seconds; 6. 1 hour, 8 minutes, 4.5 seconds – Suggested answer: Because the time would be 1/2 the total amount, take 1/2 of 2 hours, 1/2 of 16 minutes, and 1/2 of 9 seconds.

Page 59

1. 1866; 2. B.; 3. 1,500 inches; 4. 10,000 + 1,000 + 300 + 60 + 8; 5. 600; 6. 7 jumps – Suggested answer: The frog manages to climb 20 feet with each jump; the 7th jump gets him out of the canyon.

Page 61

1. D.; 2. 116 inches; 3. 11 years; 4,015 days; 4. 65 days; 5. greater than; 6. 9 feet 8 inches – 7 feet 6 inches = 2 feet 2 inches; 9 2/3 feet – 7 1/2 feet = 2 1/6 feet; 116 inches – 90 inches = 26 inches

Page 63

1. June 2007; 2. human hair ball, plastic wrap ball, aluminum foil ball, and rubber band ball; 3. A.; 4. about 60 pounds; 5. 5 feet 3 inches; 6. The human hair ball would weigh more – Suggested answer: A 12-foot ball of human hair would weigh about 501 pounds; the 11.5-foot plastic wrap ball weighs only 281.5 pounds.

Page 65

1. 5,632 ounces; 2. 1/2 minute; 3. 928 pounds; 4. $171.60; 5. 429 soft drink cans would weigh more by 34.5 pounds; 6. Answers will vary, but the total weight of the items in the set should equal 352 pounds. Two examples are 2 people, 10 bricks, 4 cans, or 1 person, 10 bricks, 204 cans.

Page 67

1. 25 feet; 2. 16,209; 25,408; 33,826; 128,089; 3. about 3 tons; 4. 1,000; 5. B.; 6. The area of the Largest Cake would be greater – Suggested answer: Its area would be 2,560 square feet (80 x 32) while the 50-foot cake's area would be 2,500 square feet (50 x 50).

Page 69

1. 17 dozen; 2. 375 7/100; 3. A.; 4. 244.57 feet; 5. 1/3 of the bun – Suggested answer: 11 pounds is 1/3 of 33 pounds; 6. less than 1/2 foot – Suggested answer: 1,000 pieces that are each 1/2-foot long would produce 500 feet, but the hot dog is only 375 feet.

Page 71

1. 3 million; 2. 2,700,000; 3. $9,400; 4. 230; 5. 7 bills: 3 50-dollar bills, 1 20-dollar bill, 1 10-dollar bill, 1 5-dollar bill, 1 1-dollar bill; 6. $88, $98 – Accept all reasonable answers. For example, a student might use the "guess-and-check" method by starting with two numbers that have a difference of 10 and adding them. Depending on the sum, the student would adjust the numbers by increasing or decreasing them.

Page 73

1. 120 seconds; 2. less than; 2.8 inches less; 3. B.; 4. 10,000 pizzas if 26,874 is rounded to 27,000; 9,000 pizzas if 26,874 is rounded to 27,000 and 2.7 is rounded to 3; 5. 4.4 ounces; 6. 355 pizzas – Suggested answer: 142 pizzas are made in the first hour, 142 are made in the second hour, and 71 are made in the last 1/2 hour.

Page 75

1. D.; 2. 240; 3. C.; 4. 119.6 square feet; 5. A.; 6. 4.6 square meters

Page 77

1. 180; 2. D.; 3. 2 minutes, 1.2 seconds; 4. C.; 5. D.

Page 79

1. A.; 2. B.; 3. It took about 5 years – Suggested answer: His hair was 4 1/2 inches in 2002, and it was 7 inches in 2007. 2007 – 2002 = 5; 4. B.; 5. yes; 6. D.

Page 81

1. 13 miles; Students' drawings should show a line labeled 12 to 13, divided into 10 parts with 12.8 marked more than halfway to 13 or at the eighth part; 2. 67,056 feet; 3. C.; 4. 349.1 inches; 5. BigDog is slightly larger than the Largest Robot Dog – Suggested answer: 32 inches is less than 3 feet, and 26 inches is just over 2 feet; 6. A little more than 3 hours – Suggested answer: Estimate by rounding the decimals to the nearest whole number. Students should estimate that the robot will travel at about 4 miles per hour. At that rate, it will take a little more than 3 hours to travel almost 13 miles.

Page 83

1. 5 feet taller; 27,000 pounds heavier; 2. 38,4000 ounces; 3. D.; 4. 64 inches; 5. 6 feet 10 inches; 6. 3 of the lighter truck and 2 of the heavier truck

Page 85

1. 2; 2. 7 1/2 (7.5) feet; 3. 44 years old; 4. 38 days; 5. B.; 6. D.

Page 87

1. C.; 2. 1; 3. 180 miles; 4. 800,000; 5. B.; 6. over 150 feet – Suggested answer: Söderman had to drive across the 10-foot-wide track to get each of the 15 cans (10 x 15 = 150). Because the cans had to be diagonally staggered, the cans were probably actually farther apart.

Page 89

1. 55; 2. D.; 3. 6.5; 4. 0.0002%; 5. D.; 6. 1,400 – Suggested answer: Assuming that each person had 2 feet and 2 armpits, divide 5,600 by 4 to get 1,400.

Page 91

1. 3; 2. 616.81; 3. A.; 4. D.; 5. B.;
6. 19,429.5 – Suggested answer: 36 is
1 1/2 times greater than 24. Multiply
the watts produced by 1.5, so (1.5)
(12,953) = 19,429.5.

Page 93

1. 6.6 inches; 2. Keisha, Wilco,
Duangdee, Adams, Kosen;
3. 4.25 inches; 4. 3 feet 5 inches;
5. 500 square feet; 6. 7

Page 95

1. $7,500; 2. $13,775,000;
3. 32 ounces; 4. $17,500,000;
5. $295,000; 6. $120,900

Page 97

1. 110 inches; 2. Yes, Yilmaz is able to
squirt milk a total of 9 feet 2 inches. –
Suggested answer: Because 12 inches
are in a foot, he can squirt milk 110
inches. Therefore, he could ignite a
candle 105 inches away; 3. 1 minute,
25 seconds; 4. 5 minutes, 12 seconds;
5. about 21 seconds – Suggested
answer: Yilmaz spent 1 minute,
44 seconds igniting 5 targets. Because
60 seconds are in 1 minute, he spent
104 seconds igniting 5 targets.
104 divided by 5 is 20.8, which rounds
to 21 seconds; 6. about 3 seconds –
Suggested answer: Anting took
17 seconds to put out 5 candles.
17 divided by 5 is 3.4, which rounds
to 3.

Page 99

1. 11 feet; 2. B.; 3. 4,284; 4. 8 feet
11 inches; 5. 30,420 pounds; 6. 12

Page 101

1. 128 inches; 2. Yes – Suggested
answer: Because it is only 8 feet
1 inch in height, the TOUGHPHONE
can survive a fall from 10 feet 8 inches;
3. 7,000 pounds; 4. No – Answers will
vary but may include: A story is about
10 feet, so the TOUGHPHONE could
not survive a 30-foot drop; 5. 32,224;
6.

2	32
4	64
6	96
8	128

Page 103

1. B.; 2. C.; 3. 167.3 ounces; 4. 20;
5. 82/ 60 = 1.37 coconuts per second;
6. About 1,440 feet. Multiply 60
seconds by 4 minutes to convert
4 minutes to seconds: (4)(60) = 240
seconds. Round amounts and set up
a proportion comparing the time to
the height: 30 feet/5 seconds = x/240
seconds. Cross-multiply 30 by 240:
(30)(240) = 7,200. Divide 7,200 by 5
(7,200/ 5) = 1,440.

Page 105

1. 30; 2. 36,511.2; 3. 57; 4. C.; 5. A.;
6. Skorkovsky – Suggested answer:
Low's rate of speed is 2.8 miles per
hour. To find Skorkovsky's rate of
speed, divide 26.219 miles by 7.25
hours (26.219/ 7.25 = 3.62 miles per
hour). Skorkovsky has the higher rate
of speed because 3.62 miles per hour
is faster than 2.8 miles per hour.

Page 107

1. 132 years (in 2010); 2. 20,000 +
7,000; 3. about 9; 4. A.; 5. 21,900 days
– Suggested answer: 1939 to 1999
equals 60 years. (60 years)(365 days
per year) = 21,900 days; 6. C.

Page 109

1. C.; 2. 821,196.8; 3. 7;
4. 79.28 pounds; 5. B.; 6. once
every 2.5 seconds

Page 111

1. 5,280; 2. 45; 3. 87.47; 4. 2 x 5 x 3
x 3; 5. D.; 6. The mode – Suggested
answer: Mode tells which amount is
most frequently juggled and would
provide the most accurate measure
of central tendency. Median would
provide only a middle amount, and
mean could be skewed by an outlier.

Page 113

1. C.; 2. 36, as of 2010; 3. 104;
4. 4; 5. Because a pole vaulter ascends
and descends at an angle, Isinbayeva's
vault covered the area of a triangle.
The formula for the area of a triangle
is A = 1/2bh (base x height). Students
should draw a triangle with a height of
16 feet 7 inches.

Page 115

1. 2005; 2. 169.17 feet or 169 feet
2 inches difference; 3. about 7 yards;
4. 73; 5. 31; 6. 9 – Suggested answer:
564 total players on 62 different
teams; 564 divided by 62 is 9.1, which
rounds to 9 players per team.

Page 117

1. 4.43; 2. 120; 3. 5.12; 4. Toe, 1 Finger,
Header, Nose; 5. 114.88 seconds;
6. 39

Page 119

1. six thousand seventy pounds;
2. 37–38 feet; 3. 1,217 pounds;
4. 384 inches; 5. 69.5; 6. $14,000

Page 121

1. 1,000 + 100 + 70 + 3; 2. Wednesday
3. 5,687 pounds; 4. 10 times; 5. about
75 pounds each; 6. 806 pounds

Page 123

1. 3, 2, 4, 1; 2. one thousand two
hundred fourteen; 3. 607; 4. C.; 5. 64;
6. about 130

Page 125

1. 11,097; 10,000 + 1,000 + 90 + 7;
2. 6,219; 3. 27 years; 4. 17; 5. 443;
6. 264